Ben Carson
Rₓ for America

JOHN PHILIP SOUSA IV

KALEIDOSCOPE PUBLISHING LTD

Kaleidoscope Publishing, Ltd.

© 2015 John Philip Sousa IV. All rights reserved.

Title is also available as a Kindle™ book through Amazon.com

Title is also available as an audio book through Amazon.com

Requests for information should be sent to Kaleidoscope Publishing, Ltd., 1420 Spring Hill Rd., #490, Tysons Corner, VA 22102; 703-821-1589; info@kaleidoscopepublishingltd.com

ISBN 978-0-9962533-1-4

Scripture used is taken from GOD'S WORD® Copyright 1995 by God's Word to the Nations. Used by permission. All rights reserved.

First softcover printing 2015

Cover photo: Max Taylor

Cover design: Andy Hall

Printed in the United States of America

This Book is dedicated to the millions of Americans of every race, color, and creed who have decided that Ben Carson is the one man who can save the America that our Founding Fathers created.

Contents

Introduction

My great grandfather, John Philip Sousa, who later became known world-wide as the *March King*, was born on November 6, 1854, just a few years prior to the American Civil War. He was a proud American. In fact, he loved everything about America—its boldness, its audacity, its can-do confidence, its reverence for the rule of law, its belief in God, and especially its heritage of freedom. He understood that the United States of America was truly an exceptional nation in the annals of history, well before that term was used to describe our country. I feel strongly that if he were alive today, he would be in the front ranks of those supporting the candidacy of Dr. Benjamin Carson for president of the United States. He would have loved Dr. Carson's compassion for his fellow man, his humility, and his clarity of vision. More than that, my great grandfather would have respected Ben Carson's commonsense values, and his dedication to the principles and ideals of America's Founders. And he would have known that in these challenging times that only a man of Ben Carson's character and wisdom could lead our nation back to greatness.

I wrote this book to introduce you to Ben Carson, his story, his vision and his character. If you plan to vote in a presidential primary, attend a presidential caucus, or will be participating in a convention that chooses delegates to the 2016 Republican National Convention, I hope you will take the time to read this book.

In fact, it is my hope that you will support Dr. Benjamin Carson, a great American with an amazing life story, strong leadership experience, incredible personal accomplishments, and a clear vision for America's future. You'll be surprised to learn of his accomplishments, his experience, and why he has what it takes to serve as president of the United States.

Benjamin Solomon Carson burst onto the political scene when he gave the keynote address at the 2013 National Prayer Breakfast. With President and Mrs. Obama sitting nearby, as well as Vice President Biden, Ben Carson boldly, yet respectfully rejected Barack Obama's plan to redistribute income and to nationalize our health care system. With the precision of a surgeon, he dissected both policies as unwise, unworkable, counterproductive, and unethical.

That one speech set off a national hue and cry for Dr. Ben Carson to run for president of the United States. Millions of Americans from coast-to-coast and border-to-border began clamoring for Ben Carson to run for president. And, thanks to the National Draft Ben Carson for President Committee, a group for which I served as chairman, they have been organized into an army of volunteers, donors, and leaders who have helped to propel Ben Carson into the ranks of frontrunners for the Republican nomination for president in 2016. Recently, the National Draft Ben Carson for President Committee changed its name to The 2016 Committee, a change required by Federal Election Commission (FEC) regulations. However, our mission remains the same, to nominate and elect Ben Carson as the next President of the United States.

Like Barry Goldwater and Ronald Reagan before him, Ben Carson has inspired countless thousands, even millions to get involved in the political process for the first time. Through the power of his public speaking and the simple eloquence of his speeches, books and newspaper columns, he has become a frontrunner for the Republican presidential nomination. He is also recognized as the leader of a movement that seeks a return to commonsense economics, honesty, constitutional practice, peace through strength, traditional values, liberty and justice for all. Ben Carson has lived the American Dream and, as president, he will make it possible for every American to have the opportunity to climb the ladder of success as far as their skill, hard work, and God's blessings take them.

I believe Ben Carson is the right choice for 2016. It is my hope that once you read this book you, too, will make Dr. Benjamin Carson your choice for president.

John Philip Sousa IV
Farmington, Connecticut
March 16, 2015

Chapter 1
Ben Carson the Man

Long before he ever came on the political scene, Dr. Carson was well known and respected around the world for his skill as a pediatric neurosurgeon. But, his becoming a ground-breaking and world renowned pediatric neurosurgeon had a most unlikely beginning.

Benjamin Solomon Carson grew up in a single family home with his mother and brother in one of the worst areas of Detroit, Michigan. They lived just a short distance from the famous Ford Rouge River Plant. It wasn't exactly a recipe for success. It fact, the outlook was bleak.

When Ben Carson was in the 5th grade, his classmates called him *"dummy"* because he had terrible grades. He also had a violent temper. He threw rocks at cars, even police cars, and then, when they stopped, dared them to chase him. He was headed down the wrong path and his situation looked hopeless.

His mother married at 13, only to find out, after having two boys, that her husband was a bigamist. Being a woman of faith, she sent her unfaithful husband packing and set about raising her two children on her own. Because she was illiterate, the only work she could find was as a domestic, cleaning the homes of others.

Sonya, Ben's mother, refused to go on welfare. She may have been illiterate, but she noticed that anyone who went on welfare never got off of welfare. She did not want that for herself or for her boys. But, things were not going well for Ben and Curtis. She knew Ben was smart, but he was always getting into trouble, and he was not doing well at school, so she prayed about it.

Sonya worked very, very hard, often working two or three jobs to provide for her boys. She was cleaning the house of a rather wealthy individual one day and noticed that the television was covered with books. She said to the gentleman, *"How do you watch television with all these books on your TV set?"* He said he would rather read books than watch TV. Sonya went home and said, *"Boys, new rule in the house. No more than one hour of television in this house. You're going to read."* ...Thanks to that one change, Ben Carson and his brother, Curtis, were pulled out of poverty and put on the road to success.

So, except for one or two favorite shows each week, Sonya turned off the television and the boys read two books per week (from the local library). In addition, even though she could not read, she required Ben and Curtis to write book reports on each book they read and give them to her. She would even mark up their reports as if she was grading them.

At first, Ben especially hated not being able to go outside with the rest of the children, and he hated reading books. But, soon he was devouring books as fast as he could read them. And, in just two years, he was the star pupil in his class. He was no longer the class dummy, he was the class brain.

In high school Ben's leadership skills blossomed, especially in the ROTC where he earned medals for his rifle marksmanship. In just three years he was promoted to the rank of Colonel after receiving the highest score ever recorded on a field grade examination. To top it off,

Carson was given the title of executive officer over all the high school ROTC programs in the Detroit public school system. In recognition of this achievement, he led the Memorial Day Parade in Detroit and met General William Westmoreland. He also had dinner with a number of Medal of Honor recipients. Most important of all, he was offered an appointment to United States Military Academy at West Point. In his own words, this is what he said about his ROTC experience...

> *"I was thrilled by the whole ROTC experience. ...it taught me a wide variety of skills. It also bolstered my confidence to believe I might find a military career quite satisfying if I accepted that scholarship to West Point."*[1]

However, after weighing his options, Ben Carson passed up the opportunity to attend West Point to pursue his dream of becoming a physician. As he put it:

> *"Not only did I remain convinced that God wanted me to become a doctor, but I had read many Bible verses telling me God would answer my fervent prayers and grant the desires of my heart. My desire was to go to Yale, and I prayed for that fervently."*[2]

Indeed, after graduating from high school with honors, he only had enough money to apply to one school, so he applied to Yale. He was accepted and attended Yale University on a scholarship. After Yale, where he met his future bride, Lacena "Candy" Rustin, he attended medical school at the University of Michigan. Ben always set his sights high. After graduation from medical school, he was hired by Johns Hopkins Hospital, one of the most prestigious teaching hospitals in the United States. When he became a neurosurgeon, there were only eight black neurosurgeons in the entire world.[3]

At the age of 33, he became the youngest major Division Director in Johns Hopkins history, responsible for running a multi-hundred million dollar enterprise.[4] Everyone recognized him as a brilliant and compassionate physician. But that was just the beginning.

In 1987 Dr. Ben Carson did something that had never before been done in world history. Leading a medical team of 70, he successfully separated twins conjoined at the head, keeping both alive. In the past, one twin had always died, but Dr. Carson developed a new technique that enabled both twins to live. Subsequently, Dr. Carson successfully led medical teams that separated 11 pairs of twins connected at the head.

As a physician, Ben Carson was known for his compassion. In spite of his intense schedule, he would take as much time as needed to talk with the parents of a patient, or the patient himself, to fully explain the procedure he was planning to undertake, and the risks involved. He patiently answered questions and did his best to reassure his patients and their parents that everything possible was being done to save their life or solve their problem. It was not uncommon for him to pray with his patients. And he always urged them to pray about the procedure the night before surgery, telling them that he would be praying about it, too.

Dr. Carson's achievements have not been limited to the operating room. When Carson and his wife, Candy, read a research study about education in the United States they were alarmed by the findings. The study showed that our nation's students ranked 21st out of 22 countries, next to the bottom of the list in science and math. In order to do something about this decline in educational performance, he and his wife, Candy, established the Carson Scholars

Fund in 1994.[5] Its purpose is to provide encouragement and support to talented young people living in poverty as well as to address the education crisis in the United States. Open to children of all backgrounds and all races, this scholarship program operates in all 50 states, and has received worldwide recognition for its successes.

The Carsons also noticed that while high school sports stars received high praise, great attention, and huge trophies, those students who excelled scholastically only received a pin or a certificate. So, in light of the study, and the lack of encouragement for students who do well in school, they established programs to celebrate and honor academic achievement.

The Carson Scholars Fund awards scholarships to students in grades four through eleven who not only excel in school, but also exhibit humanitarian qualities. Scholarship winners receive a $1,000 scholarship toward a college education, and recognition that includes attendance at an awards banquet. The objective is to make these top performing students role models at their schools.

The second program of the foundation started in 2000 and consists of creating attractive Ben Carson Reading Rooms all across the nation. The goal is to encourage young children to read. Carson understood that reading is the key to learning and knew it was the reason for his success in school and ultimately becoming a medical doctor. Today there are more than 110 of these reading rooms across the nation.

For nearly two decades Dr. Carson has served on the Board of Directors of two multinational corporations, the Kellogg Company and Costco. In 2001, Dr. Carson was named one of the nation's foremost scientists and physicians by *Time* magazine and CNN. Also in 2001, the

Library of Congress selected him as one of the nation's 89 *"Living Legends."* In 2006, the NAACP awarded Carson its highest honor, the Spingarn Medal. Carson was also the recipient of the Horatio Alger Award, whose other recipients include Bob Dole, Dwight Eisenhower, Gerald Ford, and Ronald Reagan. The Horatio Alger Award is given to *"...extraordinary self-made Americans."*[6] For his brilliance, his leadership, and his compassion, Dr. Carson was awarded the Presidential Medal of  Freedom in 2008, the nation's highest civilian award.[7] Ben Carson has also been awarded thirty-eight honorary doctorate degrees.[8] A December 2014 Gallup poll found that Dr. Ben Carson is the sixth most admired man in America.[9] No other prospective Republican candidate for president made it into the top ten of this prestigious listing. Another Gallup poll revealed that Ben Carson is the only Republican candidate for president who is more popular with the American people than Hillary Clinton.[10] He is also a *New York Times* best-selling author of seven books, his book, *One Nation*, released about the same time as Hillary Clinton's highly touted biography *Hard Choices*, far outsold the Clinton book and was on the *New York Times* nonfiction bestseller list for five weeks.

A major motion picture starring Cuba Gooding, Jr., was released in 2009 about the life of Ben Carson. The movie, *"Gifted Hands,"*[11] describes his upbringing, his early anger, his triumph over anger, and his medical successes. The movie was particularly well-received by African Americans who have been aware of the doctor's many accomplishments for years. Young African Americans have been told the amazing story of Ben Carson for generations. Dr. Carson has been used as a role model by parents to encourage their children to work hard, overcome challenges, get a good education, and achieve the American Dream. It is not an exaggeration to say that Dr. Ben Carson is revered in the African American community, especially by people of faith.

How respected and highly regarded is Dr. Ben Carson? Even those who disagree with him on public policy issues speak glowingly of his achievements and his character. For instance, the endorsements on the back of the book *Gifted Hands* include these warm words...[12]

"Some say he would be a great man even if he never picked up a scalpel."—Parade Magazine
*"He works miracles on children others have written off as hopeless."—*Barbara Walters

As noted in the Introduction, Dr. Ben Carson erupted onto the political scene as a result of his speech at the 2013 National Prayer Breakfast.[13] Prior to that event, Dr. Carson and his wife, Candy, had co-authored the book, *America the Beautiful*, which expressed his concerns for the future of our nation. But, it was not until he spoke at the National Prayer Breakfast, with President and Mrs. Obama, along with Vice President Biden sitting nearby, that the public truly took note of Dr. Carson's political views and his ability to explain complicated issues in simple terms.

In that speech, Ben Carson respectfully, yet directly, addressed the dangers of a growing National Debt to future generations. He also talked about the non-Biblical idea of income and wealth re-distribution. And, finally, he gently suggested that there was a better approach to universal health care other than the Affordable Care Act (aka

Obamacare) that would be less costly, less intrusive, less bureaucratic and would not put the government between a patient and his doctor. Dr. Carson called for Obamacare to be replaced by a health savings account program that would strengthen the patient-doctor relationship and eliminate the need for a massive new government bureaucracy. He realized that Obamacare would grant unprecedented power to the federal government and ultimately reduce the freedom of American citizens. He later wrote of the move to government run health care...

"I think this shift is beginning to wrench the nation from one centered on the rights of individual citizens to one that accepts the right of the government to control even the most essential parts of our lives. This strikes a serious blow to the concept of freedom that gave birth to this nation."[14]

While the White House was angry about Ben Carson's speech at the 2013 National Prayer Breakfast, the response of the American people was an outpouring of support greater than for any speech since Ronald Reagan's *"Time for Choosing"* speech.[15] More than 4.3 million people have viewed Carson's National Prayer Breakfast speech on YouTube™. That was the beginning of a coast-to-coast, border-to-border outcry for Dr. Carson to run for president of the United States.

Chapter 2
Why Ben Carson Will Win

Why is Ben Carson the one candidate who is sure to win the White House in 2016? It is not just that he is likely to win a large share of the African American vote, the Hispanic vote, and the Asian vote. Nor is it just that he is blessed with a Reaganesque ability to communicate with everyday Americans on complex and complicated issues in simple terms that everyone can understand. It is all of those things, but it is more than that.

The fact is, poll after poll shows that Americans from coast-to-coast and border-to-border are weary of slick politicians in both political parties. They seek someone they can trust, and they especially want someone of unimpeachable character. They are leery of politicians that cut ethical corners, and think that they are smarter than the citizens who elected them. They desperately want a president who is not only committed to the United States Constitution and to freedom, they want a man of faith and traditional values who understands that at its core, the greatest challenge facing our nation is spiritual in nature. All these problems—economic, domestic, foreign policy— are all caused by an accelerating moral crisis. Our judges, our appointed officials, our legislators, and yes, our president is failing because they have lost their moral compass. The greatest attribute of the man who held our nation together during the darkest times of the American Revolution, George Washington, was his character. George Washington's moral compass never failed him. It was what enabled him to persevere and lead, even when it seemed that there was no hope. It enabled him to triumph without grasping power, even when that opportunity was presented to him.

Americans want a leader who has the character to tell the truth, even when it is not politically advantageous to do so. They want someone who will take responsibility for his failures, and they want a president who understands that he is a servant of the people, not their master. That man is Ben Carson. And, because he is a man of character, he has that one single attribute that you can't buy, you can't borrow, and you can't get through education and success—trustworthiness. Americans trust Ben Carson because he has led an exemplary life of achievement without compromising his values. Trust is the single greatest attribute the American people seek in a candidate for president. They don't want a schemer, a prevaricator, or another politician. They want a man who says what he means and means what he says. That's the kind of man Ben Carson is and has always been.

Yes, it is true that the nomination of Ben Carson will make it possible for the Republican Party to reclaim the historic level of support accorded to previous Republican candidates for president by the African American community. It will also enable the GOP to win a large share, perhaps a majority, of the Hispanic and the Asian vote.

Why is winning a large share, perhaps a majority, of the minority vote important, other than the fact that conservative solutions benefit all Americans?

Historically, the Republicans have been champions of the poor and oppressed. From the time of Abraham Lincoln until the election of Franklin D. Roosevelt, black Americans overwhelmingly supported Republican candidates for president. Understandably, as the party of slavery, segregation, racism and white supremacy, the Democrat Party had great difficulty in winning over black voters. Blacks shifting their support to Roosevelt is not without its irony. It was President Franklin D. Roosevelt who appointed a member of the Ku Klux Klan, Hugo Black, to the United States Supreme Court.[16] Yet, it was during Roosevelt's extended term in office that African Americans began to shift toward supporting Democrat candidates. Although the shift began in the 1930s, it really was not complete until 1964, when Barry Goldwater ran for president and received less than 10% of the African American vote. In fact, in 1956, Dwight Eisenhower won 39% of the black vote and, in 1960, Richard Nixon won nearly 30% of the African American vote when they ran for president.

The GOP disconnected from African Americans when Barry Goldwater, an early civil rights supporter, voted against the 1964 Civil Rights Act on the grounds that it was unconstitutional.[17] Goldwater had previously voted for every Civil Rights Act, while his opponent in 1964, Lyndon Johnson, had, as a United States Senator, voted against every Civil Rights Act. Nevertheless, Goldwater's vote was the tipping point that caused the final mass exodus of African Americans from the Republican Party.

Yet today polls still show that 37% of African Americans identify themselves as conservative, while only 36% identify themselves as liberal.[18] And, when asked about issues such as abortion, taxes, school vouchers, national defense and traditional marriage, these black Americans come down firmly on the conservative side. But, contrary to reality, they continue to identify the Democrat Party as the party that stands with them on these issues. Finally, being convinced that all Republicans and conservatives are racists, they vote as an almost solid bloc for Democrat candidates. In fact, in 2012, Mitt Romney received just 7% of the black vote. It was a historic low point of support for Republican presidential candidates.

It is difficult to understand this disconnect between conservative African Americans and the Republican Party. Nevertheless, this disconnect is a reality, and it is the reason that black Americans shy away from voting for Republican candidates. Even though they are philosophical soulmates of most Republican candidates in regard to support for low taxes, school vouchers, life, a strong national defense and traditional values, they continue to vote for their Democrat opponents who oppose almost everything they believe in. What is it that causes this disconnect? The answer is trust. Black conservatives simply do not trust Republicans and conservatives. They are convinced that Republicans, especially conservatives, are racist. It's not surprising that conservative black Americans believe such a lie. After all, that's what they read each day in the newspaper and hear on television. Their lack of trust has been fostered by the Democrat Party and their allies in the national news media. And, practically speaking, a bond of trust once broken is very difficult to restore, especially when the media continues to portray Republicans as racists.

Restoring the historic bond of trust that black Americans have had with the GOP is a challenge that must be overcome if the Republican Party is to become successful on a continuing basis. However, just running a black candidate will not automatically restore this broken bond of trust, unless that candidate has previously established a bond of trust that has existed for many decades prior to his or her running for office. That is what makes nominating Ben Carson such a great opportunity for Republicans and conservatives. He has a unique and revered standing in the African American community that will be very difficult to tarnish.

As noted in the first chapter, Ben Carson was the 2006 recipient of the NAACP's highest award, the Spingarn Medal (previously given to such luminaries as Oprah Winfrey, Colin Powell, Jackie Robinson, Rosa Parks, Hank Aaron and many more), and he was the subject of a full-length movie, "*Gifted Hands*," that told the story of his incredible medical accomplishments. He has been feted on countless national television programs such as the "*Today Show*." Indeed, Dr. Benjamin Carson is an icon in the African American community. He is a man whose word is trusted by black Americans all across our nation. In fact, he is revered by Americans of every race and background, but especially by African Americans.[19] In other words, Ben Carson's bond of trust among blacks and Hispanics is broad and deep. They know his name. They have heard his story. They know of his success. It is one thing to claim that you are a friend; it is altogether something else to have expressed your friendship through word and deed over a long period of time. That is the case with Dr. Ben Carson who is the one candidate who can connect with black and Hispanic voters, winning their confidence and their vote. Ben Carson is trusted by these voters who have been too long ignored by the Republican Party.

Trust is the bottom line. Whether it is a contract, a marriage, a friendship or a business relationship, trust is the essential ingredient. Every treaty negotiated by a president is based on mutual trust. For an entrepreneur to be successful, he must be trusted by his clients and customers. In order for you to place your money in a bank, you must trust that it is solvent and that it will protect your funds. And, once broken, trust is very difficult to restore. It takes patience, humility, energy, and in the case of politics, a long term example of reliability and trustworthiness. Trust is the only plausible explanation of why the internal polls of the Herman Cain campaign showed him winning such a large share of the African American vote, even while running against a black incumbent president.[20]

Although it is untrue that the leaders of the Democrat Party are the friends of African Americans and Hispanics, and that the Republicans are their enemies, the Democrats, and their allies in the news media, have effectively destroyed any bond of trust that should exist today. Sadly, even though there are many opportunities to appeal to black and Hispanic voters on common issues, those appeals will fall on deaf ears as long as no bond of trust exists between those communities and the Republican Party or its candidates.

Think about it. If I do not trust Republicans to do what they say they will do, why would I even consider voting for them? It makes no sense to do so. If you don't trust a carpenter to do a good job, you don't hire him, no matter how low his price, or how much he assures you that he will do a good job. Trust is the reason that Angie's List™ is successful.[21] Why do you look for someone to work on your house that gets a high rating on Angie's List? You do it because you believe you can trust that tradesman to perform as promised.

Trust is the foundational reason people enter into contracts. And, it is the reason that more Hispanics and African Americans vote for Democrat candidates. A lack of trust is the chief barrier to black and Hispanic Americans voting for Republicans.

The reality is that if the Republican presidential nominee does not have a solid base of trust in minority communities BEFORE he runs for president, he is not going to win their votes. In the case of Dr. Ben Carson, he earned that bond of trust in the black community many years ago. He has been there for African Americans when they needed him. And, as president, he will create the environment and the opportunity for millions of black, Hispanic, Asian, and white Americans to escape poverty.

It is not surprising that both President George W. Bush and President Barack Obama offered the position of Surgeon General to Dr. Carson.[22] They both understand the universal high regard in which Dr. Carson is held among Americans of all races and ethnic backgrounds.

Taking that fact into consideration, just imagine how successful Ben Carson would be running against Hillary Clinton or any other Democrat Party nominee. And, it is conceivable, perhaps likely, that he would win in a landslide.

Dr. Carson's high standing in the black community, and particularly with Christians, has existed for many years. Those African Americans who attend churches are very familiar with the story of Dr. Benjamin Carson.

Respect for Ben Carson is very broad and deep in the African American community. A measurement of that breadth and depth was shown when the far left Southern Poverty Law Center (SPLC) placed Ben Carson on their "hate" list. African Americans, a large number who were supporters the SPLC, were outraged by this affront to one of their most cherished leaders. After what the Southern Poverty Law Center described as *"intense criticism"* from their black supporters, they not only removed Ben Carson's name from their hate list, but publicly apologized to him.[23] Ben Carson's support in the African American community is not only broad, it also includes recognized and respected leaders like Dr. Alveda King, the niece of Dr. Martin Luther King, Jr. Dr. Alveda King served in the Alabama legislature as a Democrat and campaigned for Jesse Jackson when he ran for president. This time she has not only endorsed the presidential candidacy of Ben Carson, but also pledged to do everything she can to elect him. You can be confident that if Ben Carson is the Republican candidate for President that many notable Africans from all walks of life—from academia, from the sports world and even from Hollywood—will publicly support him in his race for the White House.

In March 2015 a national survey was conducted by The Polling Company on behalf of The 2016 Committee.[24] After reminding the African American poll participants of Dr. Carson's background and his stand on the issues, it posed this question:

"Dr. Ben Carson is an African-American who may run for President in 2016. Would you consider voting for him?"

When you exclude the maybe category, as well as the do not know and refused to answer participants, Ben Carson polls 54% of the African Americans who said yes or no in the survey. That's right, 54%!

I have witnessed the popularity of Ben Carson with African Americans first hand. In early December of 2014, I was checking out of a hotel in Philadelphia and I gave my valet ticket to a middle aged black parking attendant. In a few minutes he returned with my car (of course, covered in Carson bumper stickers) and said to me, *"I didn't know Dr.*

Carson was running for president." I said, *"He is not, but we are trying to convince him to run."*

Then I asked the gentleman, *"Are you familiar with Dr. Carson?"*

He smiled and said that he did and *"As a matter of fact, not a week goes by that my wife and I don't talk to our kids about Dr. Carson and his background...we tell our kids that if Dr. Carson can be a success, you certainly can, too".*

I then asked the man if he would support Dr. Carson for president and his face lit up like a Christmas tree. It was obvious that he and his wife would be delighted to vote for Ben Carson.

This is the kind of respect and standing that someone must have in the African American community prior to any involvement in politics if they hope to receive strong support from black Americans. Such long-term respect creates a nearly unbreakable bond of trust that will allow Ben Carson to win over black and Hispanic Americans to the Republican ticket in 2016. And, when that trust is backed up by performance that proves that he stands with them on conservative issues, the bond of trust that currently exists with the Democrat Party will be shattered for good.

There is one more thing that gives Ben Carson credibility in the black community, and that is the fact that he has *"blood in the soil."*[25] He is the first presidential candidate in history to be able to make that claim. This expression is used within the African American community and it holds a very strong meaning for them. It means that a person is a descendent of slaves. In fact, it was because Barack Obama does not have *"blood in the soil"* that the African American community was slow to rally behind him in 2008. And, of great significance to black Americans, Ben Carson would be the first descendent of slaves to sit in the Oval Office. This would give the black community a unique sense of pride that would be above and beyond that which exists for Barack Obama.

As further testimony of the universal esteem in which Dr. Carson is held by African Americans, consider these words from, of all people, Jesse Jackson...

"He is a model for all the youth of today."[26]

That's right, even Jesse Jackson, a man who definitely sides with the Democrats, respects and admires Ben Carson. Nominating Dr. Ben Carson will send a powerful message to the black community that one of their most respected heroes has now joined the ranks of Republicans. It says to African Americans, *"You know who he is; you know of his compassion, you know of his achievements, and you know you can trust him."* Nominating Ben Carson would cause both black and Hispanic voters to listen to him. African Americans and Hispanics will give Ben Carson an opportunity to make his case for their votes. By voting for Ben Carson, many will be voting for their long time hero and role model. They know his word is good. They know he is a man who can be trusted to do what he says. And, they know he's not just another politician.

It is true that Hispanics do not have the depth of knowledge or length of relationship that African Americans have had with Ben Carson. However that same national survey conducted in March of 2015 that showed 54% of African Americans would consider voting for Ben Carson also showed that 60% of Hispanics surveyed would consider voting for him. This is not surprising when you consider that Hispanics do not have a long-standing animosity for Republicans that black Americans have.

The very fact that Ben Carson escaped poverty to live the American dream and become a famous doctor places him in a positive light with aspiring Hispanics. They know that Ben Carson can identify with their own economic situation. They trust that the policies and administration of President Ben Carson will help open the doors to their own personal success and that of their children. And, since according to polls, 80% of whites, blacks, Asians, and Hispanics trust medical doctors, Carson has already established a bond of trust with them.[27]

The final thing that gives Ben Carson unique standing in the black and Hispanic communities is that he was never a Republican until it became necessary in order to run as a Republican candidate for president. In fact, during the Clinton years he became disenchanted with both political parties. This is what he wrote...

"Over the years, I found that no political party really represented my views of fairness, decency, and adherence to the principles set forth by the United States Constitution in 1787. So I became a registered Independent..."[28]

African Americans and Hispanic Americans will readily identify with this position, especially those black and Hispanic Americans who believe in traditional values, common sense, modesty, and hard work. They, along with Dr. Carson, share his distrust of both Republican and Democrat elected officials who have not been faithful to the principles of the United States Constitution.

Ben Carson himself experienced the same misgivings about the Republican Party that most African Americans and Hispanics have today. In short, he didn't trust Republicans to do what they say. This is the story he tells about why he voted for Jimmy Carter instead of Ronald Reagan...

> *"Although Reagan's logical approach to many of our social and international problems appealed to me, he was a Republican. Because of my bias in favor of the Democratic Party, I figured Reagan must, by definition, be greedy, selfish, and callous toward the poor."*[29]

In other words, Ben Carson was then just like many black and Hispanic Americans are today, distrustful of all Republicans. He liked what Reagan had to say, but believed what the Democrats said about him, that he was a bad person. However, Ben Carson eventually learned the truth...

> *"As I got to know more Republicans and conservatives, however, I came to realize that many of my political beliefs were based on nothing other than propaganda, and that there were just as many decent Republicans as there were decent Democrats."*[30]

Who could possibly be more effective in communicating the truth about conservatives and the Republican Party to black and Hispanic Americans than a man who himself distrusted conservatives and Republicans? Who else could possibly convince these voters to defect from the Democrat Party and its false promises to vote for a Republican candidate for president?

Black and Hispanic voters understand that Ben Carson has overcome the same obstacles, the same biases, the same challenges that they have faced. They believe him. They trust him. And many, if not most, African Americans and Hispanics will vote for him on Election Day 2016. He will start with that base of 37% of African Americans who self-identify themselves as conservatives and work up the ladder from there. Ben Carson will call black Americans back to their historic home in the Republican Party, and many, if not most, will answer his call.

The Republican Party has two choices. It can either slowly rebuild its relationship with African Americans over a period of decades, or it can fast-forward that relationship by selecting Ben Carson as its nominee for president in 2016. If it chooses to do neither, it risks going the way of the dinosaur.

By nominating Ben Carson, the GOP can re-connect with African Americans. The results of national survey conducted by The Polling Company alluded to earlier showing that 54% of African Americans will consider voting for Ben Carson convinces me that the Republican Party has a historic opportunity to win over black voters in numbers not seen since Dwight Eisenhower ran for president in 1952.[31] That survey also shows that nominating Ben Carson will give the GOP an opportunity to win a very sizable share of the Hispanic vote.[32] Later I will describe the actual methods by which these conservative African Americans can be won over to become reliable Republican voters. But, we don't have to wait twenty or thirty years to win a large share, perhaps a majority of the black and Hispanic vote. With Ben Carson at the top of the ticket, a man who is almost universally trusted in the African American community, the Republicans can win a large share of the African American and Hispanic vote in 2016!

Remember, in 2012, internal polling by the Herman Cain campaign indicated that Cain was backed by more than 40% of African Americans and by more than 60% of Hispanic Americans.[33] The Cain campaign was astounded and frankly puzzled by these numbers. How could Herman

Cain be supported so strongly by the African American and Hispanic American communities when he would be running against a black incumbent president, Barack Obama? It didn't seem to make any sense. Their conclusion was that a large number of both African Americans and Latinos identified with Herman Cain's life experience and hoped to escape poverty and achieve success like he did. Apparently Herman Cain was a role model whose success they sought to emulate.

There's no doubt about it, Herman Cain is well-liked in the African American community. He escaped poverty to become very successful in the business world, and his parents brought him up as a Bible believing Christian. But, even Herman Cain would not argue that he does not have the status or trust in the black community that Ben Carson possesses.

In 2014, the National Draft Ben Carson for President Committee tested the political drawing power of the Ben Carson name with black and Hispanic voters. The Committee spent $312,000 on North Carolina radio ads run on black and Spanish speaking radio stations urging these voters to vote for Thom Tillis, the Republican candidate for U.S. Senate.[34] The ads all closed with this line...

"Ben Carson trusts Thom Tillis. You should too."

Why did the National Draft Ben Carson for President Committee (now The 2016 Committee) run these ads? The reason was that in October 2014, Dr. Carson said that his decision to run would hinge on the GOP capturing control of the U.S. Senate.

It now appears that the Committee's money was well spent. By all indications, the radio ads the Committee ran in North Carolina provided the margin of victory to Thom

Tillis. In 2008, when Senator Elizabeth Dole was running for re-election, she lost the race because she only received 1% of the black vote. Two months prior to the 2014 election, that was exactly the same percentage of black Americans supporting Thom Tillis for U.S. Senate. However, as the ads kept running, support from the African American community for Tillis continued to climb. By Election Day, they hit 11.9% statewide.[35]

Interestingly, this happened even though the Committee was financially unable to run ads in the Northern crescent and the Southern tier of North Carolina where there is a heavy concentration of black voters. Nevertheless, Thom Tillis still won 11.9% of the African American vote statewide.

On election eve, prior to any election returns coming in, Bob Beckel (reporting on the *Fox News Channel*) blurted out, *"I'm reading an exit poll from North Carolina, and it says that Thom Tillis won 18% of the black vote. That can't be right!"*[36] It now appears that it was right, at least in the polling area where that exit poll was taken.

The ads run by the National Draft Ben Carson for President Committee reached approximately two-thirds of all African American voters in North Carolina. If you do the math and assume that Thom Tillis won only 1% of the black vote in the areas not reached by the ads and won 18% of the vote in the areas where two-thirds of African Americans lived the statewide black vote for Tillis would have been approximately 12%. That is the exact total of the vote that he won in the final tally.

The bottom line is that the Committee's ads moved black voters dramatically toward the Republican candidate for U.S. Senate, persuading them that incumbent Senator Kay Hagen did not support their interests.

And, since Thom Tillis won by a razor thin margin, less than 2%, it appears that the Committee's ads made the difference.

Now, if Thom Tillis can win as much as 18% of the black vote and Herman Cain was winning more than 40% of the black vote in 2012, isn't it logical to conclude that Ben Carson, who has been an icon in the black community for decades, would be even more successful than Herman Cain?

But, suppose Ben Carson receives just 17% of the black vote. Did you know that if he receives just 17% of the black vote and 40% of the Hispanic vote, it becomes mathematically impossible for Hillary Clinton or any other Democrat to win in 2016?

Of course, no candidate for president deserves our support just because he or she can win. As we shall see, however, Ben Carson may well be the most prepared, the most principled, and the most capable candidate the GOP can nominate and run for president in 2016. On top of that, he is the one candidate for president who is sure to win!

That confidence is founded upon extensive baseline testing and on the surprising support that Herman Cain received when he ran for president in 2012.

But, we'll look deeper at Ben Carson's presidential bid later. Suffice it to say, that by winning a very large share of the black and Hispanic vote, it becomes very difficult for any Democrat to win the White House.

Of course, Democrat politicians know this. They know that they must win nearly all of the black vote and nearly 75% of the Hispanic vote to win the White House. That's why they fear Ben Carson more than any other candidate. They know that their grasp on power is hanging by the thread of the despicable lie that all conservatives are racists. Today they use the words conservative and racist interchangeably.

In the 2014 election we saw shameful attempts to play the race card. In Georgia, for example, the Republican nominee for U.S. Senate, businessman David Perdue, was the subject of vicious and dishonest advertising in the black community. The Georgia Democrat Party endeavored to scare black voters by linking Perdue to the Ferguson, Missouri, police officer shooting of an unarmed young black man.[37] Fortunately, this smear effort by Democrat operatives backfired. Nevertheless, the leaders of the Democrat Party have shown that they will go to extreme lengths to *"spike"* the black vote in crucial elections, by demonizing Republicans.

It's no wonder most black voters, and many Hispanic voters, do not trust Republicans. For too many years Republicans have ignored these voters, and the result is that black and Hispanic voters have heard only one side of the story when it comes to conservative Republican candidates. The good news is that while minority voters may not trust any other Republican candidate, they have confidence in Dr. Ben Carson. For nearly three decades, before he ever talked about politics in public, they have respected and admired Ben Carson.

But, make no mistake about it, the attacks on Ben Carson as the Republican nominee for president will be vicious, unrelenting, and mean. Recently, an *American Thinker* blog warned...

"In the coming months expect a political assassination initiative against Dr. Carson that will cause 'Palinization' and the Herman Cain political assassination to pale.[38]"

So fearful are progressives that their lie that Republicans and conservatives are racist will be exposed as a fraud, they reserve their most poisonous venom for conservative African Americans like Ben Carson. For the Democrat politicians, politics means power, and they will fight like a cornered tiger to stay in power. Letting Ben Carson win the White House would forever destroy their false narrative that conservatives and Republicans are racists. It would also derail their dream of turning the United States of America into a top down socialist state.

Yes, the Democrats and their allies in the mainstream news media will do their best to smear and slander Ben Carson as a traitor to his race. They will say that because he has become successful he is out-of-touch with African Americans and Hispanics. They may even call him an *"Uncle Tom"*[39] or an *"Oreo"*[40] but, as the failed attack on Ben Carson by the Southern Poverty Law Center proved, it won't stick. Such attacks will be hard to swallow in regard to a man who has never forgotten his roots, and done so much personally to increase educational opportunities for black and Hispanic Americans through his foundation.[41] Ben Carson's actions match his words. That is the reason he has been held in such high regard by these communities for many decades. All he must do is to tell the truth and tell his own story. As Shakespeare wrote, *"...at the length truth will out."*[42]

The left's fear and venom were on public display as they launched vicious personal attacks on Associate Supreme Court Justice Clarence Thomas during his confirmation hearings. And, as the number of black Republican office holders continues to grow, the intensity of attacks on them by the left will increase. In the 2014 election, the Republican Party made history by electing the first black Republican woman to Congress, Mia Love. It also elected the first popularly elected African American Congressman from Texas, Will Hurd. And, perhaps more significant, it elected the first black man to serve in both the House of Representatives and the United States Senate, as well as being the first popularly elected African American Senator from South Carolina, Tim Scott. Shamefully, not one word of these historic elections was made by the NAACP. If Dr. King was alive he would certainly be celebrating these election victories, and he would be aghast at the partisan attitude of the NAACP. Today's NAACP seems to simply be an appendage of the Democrat Party.

Speaking of partisan attitudes and vicious attacks, who can forget the infamous article in *USA Today* by Julianne Malveaux who expressed hope that Associate Supreme Court Justice Clarence Thomas would succumb to an early death?[43] Or even the Public Broadcasting System (PBS) firing of liberal journalist Juan Williams, who had the temerity to speak out on the *Fox News Channel* expressing his concern about young, turban wearing Middle Eastern men boarding an airplane he was riding shortly after 9/11?[44] And let's not forget about the attacks on comedian Bill Cosby, when he spoke out about welfare moms who did not control and discipline their children, suggesting that they are the ones responsible for their sons and daughters taking the wrong path in life?[45] And we can't ignore the scathing verbal assaults on Walter Williams, Thomas Sowell, Shelby Steele and many, many others, including Dr. Ben Carson. This is just a small sampling of some of the outrageous insults that have come Dr. Carson's way since he spoke at the 2013 National Prayer Breakfast...

"...he's got intellectual tumors in his mind..."[46]

*"Carson is a monster...and should stay in the
operating room."47*
*"Sadly, he'll continue to be the worst thing that
happened to us since he opened his mouth."48*

Why are African American conservatives subject to
such wild and histrionic attacks by the left? Why do
liberals become unhinged when a conservative black
American speaks out or gets elected to public office? The
last comment about Ben Carson being *"...the worst thing
that happened to us since he opened his mouth"* explains
the fear of the left.49 Yes, indeed, Ben Carson will be the
worst thing that happened to the Democrat Party and to
the left. The left well understands the high regard with
which Dr. Carson is held in the African American
community. They know that he is trusted and loved by
millions of black Americans. They rightly fear that their
attacks on Ben Carson will fall on deaf ears. And, in their
heart, they know that if Ben Carson is the Republican
nominee for president in 2016, he will win, no matter who
they run for president. That's why they practically become
unhinged at the very thought of Ben Carson becoming the
Republican nominee for president.

For the Democrats, especially black Democrat
politicians, it is a matter of political survival. There is no
group of Americans that threatens the survival of the
Democrat Party more than black conservatives such as Dr.
Benjamin Carson. Black Democrats are particularly fearful
of a Carson nomination. There is no other group of elected
officials that is so out of touch with their constituency as
African American office holders. While polls show that a
large number of black Americans want low taxes, school
choice, a strong national defense, a secure border, and less

abortion, their political leaders take an opposing view on these issues.[50]

And while at least 37% of African Americans agree with conservative Republicans on the issues, they have been persuaded to believe that all conservatives are racists. Understandably, they can't make themselves vote for a Republican candidate. But, when that conservative message is carried by a black Republican, liberal black leaders are understandably threatened. Quite simply, black conservatives threaten the unjustified monolithic political grip that the Democrat Party has on the black community.

Why can we be confident that the attacks on Ben Carson will fall on deaf ears? Let's go back to the attacks on the character of Clarence Thomas when he was nominated to serve on the United States Supreme Court. That's when the true colors of the Democrat Party were revealed for everyone to see. Their racist attacks were shocking for their meanness and severity. Clarence Thomas accurately described the attacks as a *"high tech lynching for uppity blacks."*[51]

Amazingly, even after the most outrageous and foul attacks on Clarence Thomas, his support in the black community remained above 60% among both men and women.[52] It was argued by Jane Mansbridge and Katherine Tate, in the pages of *Political Science & Politics*, that this strong support for Justice Thomas was based on a perception by African Americans that the senatorial confirmation hearings for Clarence Thomas amounted to an attack on the character of a black man who had been nominated for a position of high honor.[53] In other words, the higher the position or office, the more likely the African American community will rally behind a black conservative candidate. Presuming Mansbridge and Tate to be correct, personal attacks on Ben Carson will also result in the black community standing up for Carson because such attacks will be perceived as an attack on the character of all black men. The Democrat leadership has a right to be terrified. Here's why...

As noted previously, if a Democrat candidate for president loses just 17% of the black vote, the race automatically becomes dead even. And, if, in addition, that candidate wins more than 40% of the Hispanic vote, he wins every swing state going away.   Remember, Mitt Romney received just 27% of the Hispanic vote. If Ben Carson is the GOP nominee, it is likely he will receive more than 40% of the Hispanic vote. Therefore, Carson winning just 17% of the black vote will be more than enough to win handily.   And, of course, the fact that Carson will be a stronger candidate and a better communicator than Romney only increases the odds that he will win in 2016.

Think about it. Clarence Thomas received 60% support from the black community, and Herman Cain's internal polls showed him winning more than 40% of the black vote and more than 60% of the Hispanic vote.[54] It would be illogical to believe that an even more revered figure in the African American community, Ben Carson, would receive less support from both black and Hispanic voters.

Realistically, candidate Carson should receive as strong or even stronger support from African Americans and Latino Americans than did Herman Cain, regardless of the personal attacks on him. In fact, such personal attacks may well backfire against the Democrats and cause a larger black vote for Ben Carson.

Why should the Republican Party pay attention to minority voters? Why shouldn't they just concentrate on winning sixty or even seventy percent of the white vote in order to win? The answer is that to follow that course of action is a dead end street that ends in disaster for the GOP.

If Ben Carson is nominated by the GOP, it is possible that the Democrat Party will be set back 20 to 30 years politically. There is absolutely no reason why Ben Carson will not return the Republican Party to its historic support from the black community, perhaps even surpassing such support. Once the lie that conservatives and Republicans are racists is exposed, it will be impossible for the Democrats to put that genie back into bottle. It is important to remember that the black community moved rapidly from voting for the Republicans to voting for the Democrats in the 1930s. Why then should it be surprising to see that community change just as dramatically again in the 21st century?

To illustrate this proposition, take a look at the table shown below. It shows just what would have happened in 2012 (a very bad Republican year) if Mitt Romney had won just 17% of the black vote in the swing states of Virginia, Florida and Ohio. Not only was there a very low Republican voter turnout, there was also no effort aimed specifically at black and Hispanic voters. In fact, as noted earlier, it would be accurate to say that the Latino support for Romney reached a historic low in 2012. The statistics in the following table are taken from U.S. Census Bureau data.[55]

Table 1

	83% of Black Vote for Obama	17% of Black Vote for Romney	Obama Total Votes	Romney Total Votes	Romney's Victory Margin
VA	593,450	121,550	1,942,140	1,950,741	8,601
FL	916,320	187,680	4,230,109	4,404,604	174,495
OH	580,170	118,830	2,827,403	2,814,906	-12,497

This table does not take into account any improvement in the Hispanic vote over 2012 when Romney received just 27% of that vote. Nevertheless, as you can see from the numbers, Virginia and Florida switch from Democrat to Republican, and Ohio is so close that a few more Hispanic votes, or a bigger voter turnout will tip the state to the GOP.

It is also worth noting that while there are still more legal immigrants from Mexico than there are from any other nation, China is now number two in immigration. In fact, in 2013, the top three immigrant nations were Mexico (135,028), China (71,798), and India (68,458).[56] What is the significance of this? Well, in the 2014 mid-term election, according to exit polls, the GOP won nearly 50% of the Asian vote.[57] This is the first time that has happened since Bob Dole ran for president in 1996. And, it is a stunning turnaround for the party that only won 26% of the Asian vote in 2012.[58] The importance of this turnaround is highlighted by the fact that immigration from Asia is growing rapidly and may soon pass that of immigration from Mexico, Central America and South America. Winning that vote will become equally important for Republican candidates for president in the years ahead.

It is essential to remember that in 2012 there were a record number of black voters. That year, 66.2% of all eligible African American voters voted. For the first time in history, the black voter participation rate outdistanced the white voter turnout rate which was 61.4%. In fact, in 2012, Romney received more than a million less votes than did Bush in 2004, and only slightly more than John McCain in 2008.[59]

Quite simply, Table 1 assumes that the Republicans would continue to fail at turning out their own base. Clearly, Romney was not a strong candidate. He was unattractive to black and Hispanic voters for a number of reasons, including the source of his wealth, his failure to campaign in black areas, the past positions of his religion on minority eligibility for leadership in The Church of Jesus Christ of the Latter-day Saints, and the wariness of evangelical voters to vote for a Mormon.

Even with these liabilities, as you can see, had Romney received just 17% of the black vote, he would have run strongly in each of these three swing states. The reality is that in order for the GOP to win the White House in 2016, it must have a strong ground game, a strong candidate, and the willingness to fight for the votes of black, Hispanic, and Asian Americans.

Let's assume that Ben Carson is the Republican nominee and he wins 37% of the black vote, the same percentage as the number of African Americans who identify themselves as conservatives in the polls. This is a very reasonable assumption based on the support that Herman Cain had in 2012 and the black support for Thom Tillis (thanks to the advertising efforts of the National Draft Ben Carson for President Committee) in 2014.

Again, we'll ignore the Hispanic vote and assume that there is no improvement in that area, even though in 2014 the Republican candidate for Governor of Texas, Greg Abbott, won 44% of the Hispanic vote. And, in that same year, a number of Republican candidates won as much as 50% of the Asian vote. Obviously, winning 40% or more of the Hispanic vote and upwards of 50% of the Asian vote is clearly within reach of Ben Carson. Nevertheless, the following table assumes that in 2016, GOP nominee Ben Carson receives just 27% of the Hispanic vote and 26% of the Asian vote (just as Romney did in 2012).[60] The only change is that Carson wins 37% of the black vote (the number of African Americans who identify themselves as conservatives according to the 2014 *Wall Street Journal* survey).[61] It also assumes that the turnout in 2016 is the same as it was in 2012 (quite low). Look at what happens in Virginia, Florida, and Ohio...

Table 2

	63% of Black Vote for Clinton	37% of Black Vote for Carson	Clinton Total Votes	Carson Total Votes	Carson's Victory Margin
VA	450,450	264,550	1,799,140	2,093,741	294,601
FL	695,520	408,480	4,009,309	4,625,404	616,095
OH	440,370	258,630	2,687,603	2,954,706	267,103

As you can see, Ben Carson wins these key swing states in a huge landslide. This is what I suggested earlier. When you have a larger turnout, and win 44% of the Hispanic vote, 50% of the Asian vote, as well as 37% of the black vote, the size of the victory is even greater. Swing states become solid Republican states and Democrat states become swing states. Winning just 37% of the black vote turns the election into a Republican landslide. Such a huge defeat would decimate the Democrat Party and force it back from the extreme left toward the center. As forecasted earlier, the nomination of Ben Carson has the potential to set the Democrat Party back for decades.

These numbers show why the nomination of Ben Carson provides such a great opportunity to the Republican Party. It is a historic chance to not only win an election, but also eradicate the lie that Republicans and conservatives are racists. The nomination and election of Ben Carson will also take a huge step toward bringing Americans back together as one people with common goals and aspirations. It will signal the end of class warfare and the beginning of a new era of unity and harmony. It can be one of our nation's finest hours.

By winning a huge, landslide victory, the GOP will be able to restore the American Dream for new generations of Americans, no matter the color of their skin or their place of origin. A Carson victory will also mean a return to Constitutional principles, traditional values and a strong, secure America.

It is clear that Ben Carson is the one candidate who can win over black and Latino voters in large numbers, thereby taking advantage of the demographic shift that is taking place in the United States. He can make that shift work to the benefit of the Republican Party, not against it.

Liberal politicians know that they are living on borrowed time. In their heart, they know that the lie they have been perpetuating that Republicans are racists and xenophobes will ultimately be exposed. That's why they are so terrified.

Needing to win more than 83% of the black vote and more than 73% of the Hispanic vote is not just about the Democrat candidate for president winning an election; it is a matter of survival for the Democrat Party. If their support from African Americans, Latinos and other minorities slips, their future goes from optimism to desperation.

How scared are the Democrat politicians? They are terrified. That's why they targeted black Republican Congressman Allen West and spent several million dollars to defeat him.[62] In spite of that targeting, West nearly won, even in a heavily Democrat district. The Democrats targeted West not because he was the most conservative Republican in the GOP, or the most powerful Republican in Congress, but *only* because he is a black conservative and was a rising star in the Republican Party. His very existence as a United States Congressman was a threat to their lie that all conservatives are racists. This is how Allen West summed it up...

> *"I'm a threat to what the Democrat Party stands for. Why would they want to attack a 51-year-old, African-American who has served in the United States military for 22 years? Been married for 23 years, has a wife who's accomplished — an MBA and a PhD — and two very exceptional daughters. Now what the heck do they want to attack that for? I think it's one simple thing. They fear that. They fear that voice and that's all there is to it, and I think that's a shame."*[63]

Allen West is right, Democrat politicians fear successful African Americans who don't kowtow to their liberal view of the world. It's important to understand that maintenance of this hideous lie is essential to the Democrats. Any reconciliation between Republicans and African Americans is completely unacceptable to them, and disastrous to their future. The last thing they want is harmony and unity in America between black and white Americans. They must continue to encourage anger and antagonism against conservatives and Republicans in order to maintain power.

And, frankly, black economic success also threatens them politically. They are fearful of the fact that today 38.4% of African Americans are comfortable inhabitants of America's middle class.[64] The Democrats have absolutely nothing to gain by African Americans climbing the economic ladder of success.

The Democrats' grasp on power that hangs by the slender thread not only hurts Republicans politically, but worse yet, holds back poor Americans from participating in the American Dream. Today, 23.5% of all African Americans live in poverty, compared with 13% of all American households who live in poverty.[65] The willingness with which the Democrats accept and even facilitate such continuing economic failure (whether intentional or unintentional) by black Americans exemplifies the disregard they have for, and the disservice they do to their black, Hispanic, and Asian supporters.

It is quite possible, even probable, that when this lie is exposed for what it is, the Democrats will be the recipients of an angry backlash from those to whom they have lied. After all, that is a natural human reaction. No one likes to be played for a fool, especially when the manipulator is claiming to be a friend. When that lie is exposed, do not be surprised if there is a dramatic shift in African American support from the Democrat Party to the Republican Party. That is the cataclysmic event that a Ben Carson candidacy is likely to precipitate.

Dr. Ben Carson has one final attribute that is unmatched by any other prospective 2016 Republican candidate for president. One of the reasons that Ronald Reagan won two landslide elections as president of the United States was his ability to speak over the news media, directly to the American people. Like Ben Carson, Reagan spoke softly, but in simple, understandable language that every American could understand. Not since Ronald Reagan has the Republican Party had an opportunity to nominate a candidate for president with the powerful communications skills of Ben Carson.

Having those skills doesn't make Ben Carson Ronald Reagan, but it's undoubtedly one of the reasons that some have referred to Ben Carson as the black Ronald Reagan. Of course, no candidate can fairly claim to be Ronald

Reagan. These are different times with different challenges and each man and woman has been created as a unique individual by God, each having his own strengths and weaknesses.

But, make no mistake about it, as Dr. Carson showed in his historic 2013 speech at the National Prayer Breakfast, he is blessed with an amazing ability to take complex issues and break them down into simple understandable terms that any American can understand. Great leaders have always been able to communicate clearly with their fellow citizens. This was not only an attribute of Ronald Reagan; it was also an attribute of Abraham Lincoln before him.

Using simple, every day terms, and clear unequivocal language, these men spoke with clarity to their fellow Americans at a critical moment in time. Their challenges were all different, the goals varied, but the words they spoke changed their lives, and that of the nation they led and loved. They spoke boldly, forcefully and inspirationally, sounding a clarion call to action.

The speech that changed Ronald Reagan's life and ultimately returned America to greatness was given on behalf of Barry Goldwater, Republican candidate for president in 1964.[66] The Goldwater campaign was struggling. The scurrilous attacks on Goldwater by the news media had successfully portrayed him as some sort of mad monster. The campaign was headed downhill.

It was at this moment that a few friends of Ronald Reagan persuaded him to make a televised speech to the nation. The Soviet Union was on the march around the globe. The United States was bogged down in a war in Southeast Asia, and the government led by Lyndon Johnson, had taken a sharp turn to the left. Government was growing; freedom was in retreat abroad and at home. The long-term future of the nation was in doubt.

When Reagan spoke, he was not a world leader, he was not even an elected official. In fact, at the time of his now famous October 27, 1964 speech, Ronald Reagan was best known as an actor. His speech was titled "*A Time for Choosing.*"[67] This speech not only changed the course of Ronald Reagan's life, it also ultimately affected the course of the United States.

Reagan's speech is almost as timely today as it was when he gave it more than 50 years ago. Here are some important excerpts from that speech...

"Last February 19th at the University of Minnesota, Norman Thomas, six-times a candidate for president on the Socialist Party ticket, said, 'If Barry Goldwater became president, he would stop the advance of socialism in the United States.' I think that's exactly what he will do."

"But as a former Democrat, I can tell you Norman Thomas isn't the only man who has drawn this parallel to socialism with the present administration, because back in 1936, Mr. Democrat himself, Al Smith, the great American, came before the American people and charged that the leadership of his Party was taking the Party of Jefferson, Jackson, and Cleveland down the road under the banners of Marx, Lenin, and Stalin. And he walked away from his Party, and he never returned until the day he died—because to this day, the leadership of that Party has been taking that Party, that honorable Party, down the road in the image of the labor Socialist Party of England."

"Those who would trade our freedom for the soup kitchen of the welfare state have told us they have a utopian solution of peace without victory. They call their policy 'accommodation.' And they say if

we'll only avoid any direct confrontation with the enemy, he'll forget his evil ways and learn to love us.   All who oppose them are indicted as warmongers. They say we offer simple answers to complex problems. Well, perhaps there is a simple answer—not an easy answer—but simple: If you and I have the courage to tell our elected officials that we want our national policy based on what we know in our hearts is morally right."

"We cannot buy our security, our freedom from the threat of the bomb by committing an immorality so great as saying to a billion human beings now enslaved behind the Iron Curtain, 'Give up your dreams of freedom because to save our own skins, we're willing to make a deal with your slave masters.'"

"You and I have the courage to say to our enemies, 'There is a price we will not pay. There is a point beyond which they must not advance. Winston Churchill said, 'The destiny of man is not measured by material computations. When great forces are on the move in the world, we learn we're spirits—not animals.'"

"You and I have a rendezvous with destiny. We'll preserve for our children this, the last best hope of man on earth, or we'll sentence them to take the last step into a thousand years of darkness."[68]

Barry Goldwater lost the election in a landslide, but the clarity and commonsense of Ronald Reagan's speech catapulted him onto the national stage. This actor and union leader became almost instantly the most recognized conservative leader in America. Two years later Ronald Reagan was elected Governor of California, the largest state in the nation. And, in 1980, he was elected president of the United States that was then in the worst economic crisis since the Great Depression. In addition, the Soviet Union was at its height of power, expanding into Africa and threatening Western Europe.

You, of course, know the rest of the story. Ronald Reagan not only returned the United States to economic prosperity, he brought down the Soviet Union through the enactment of the Reagan Doctrine, thus winning the Cold War *"without firing a shot,"* as his friend, British Prime Minister Margaret Thatcher said.[69]

But, without that one timely speech in 1964, Ronald Reagan would have never entered the political scene, and the United States of America would not have experienced the economic renaissance he ushered in. Moreover, it is likely that the Soviet Union would still exist, and millions of Eastern Europeans would still be enslaved. That was the power of that one speech by Ronald Reagan.

In similar fashion, and as noted in the Introduction, in the spring of 2013, a doctor by the name of Ben Carson was asked to give the keynote address at the National Prayer Breakfast. It was a very unusual invitation because only one other man, Billy Graham, had ever been asked to speak to the National Prayer Breakfast a second time.

Although President and Mrs. Obama, along with Vice President Biden, were also on the dais, for a few important minutes, the spotlight was on Dr. Ben Carson. He came to the breakfast concerned about the future of his nation. He had no notes, but he spoke boldly, courageously and yet respectfully from the heart. In his speech Ben Carson said in part...

"I think particularly about ancient Rome. Very powerful. Nobody could even challenge them militarily, but what happened to them? They destroyed themselves from within. Moral decay, fiscal irresponsibility. They destroyed themselves. If you don't think that can happen to America, you

get out your books and you start reading, but you know, we can fix it."

"I think about these problems all the time, and my role model was Jesus. He used parables to help people understand things. And one of our big problems right now, and like I said, I'm not politically correct, so I'm sorry, but you know our deficit is a big problem. Think about it. ...our National Debt [is] 16.5 trillion dollars – you think that's not a lot of money? I'll tell you what! Count one number per second...You know how long it would take you to count to 16 trillion? 507,000 years – more than a half a million years to get there. We have to deal with this.

"What about our taxation system? [It's] so complex there is no one who can possibly comply with every jot and tittle of our tax system. If I wanted to get you, I could get you on a tax issue. That doesn't make any sense. What we need to do is come up with something that is simple."

"When I pick up my Bible, you know what I see? I see the fairest individual in the universe, God, and He's given us a system. It's called tithe. Now we don't necessarily have to [make] it 10% but it's [the] principle. He didn't say, if your crops fail, don't give me any tithes. He didn't say, if you have a bumper crop, give me triple tithes. So there must be something inherently fair about proportionality. You make 10 billion dollars you put in a billion. You make $10 you put in $1... now some people say, that's not fair because it doesn't hurt the guy who made 10 billion dollars as much as the guy who made $10. Where does it say you have to hurt the guy? He's just put in a billion in the pot. We don't need to hurt him."

"And I [want to] close with this story: two hundred years ago this Nation was involved in a war, the

War of 1812. [The British] were winning that war and marching up the Eastern seaboard, destroying city after city, destroying Washington D.C., [they] burned down the White House. [Their] next stop was Baltimore. As they came into the Chesapeake Bay, there were armadas of [British] war ships as far as the eye could see. It was looking grim. Fort McHenry [was] standing right there [blocking their way to Baltimore]. General Armistead, who was in charge of Fort McHenry, had a large American flag commissioned to fly in front of the Fort. The Admiral in charge of the British Fleet was offended. [He] 'said take that flag down. You have until dusk to take that Flag down. If you don't take it down, we will reduce you to ashes.'"

"There was a young, amateur poet on board by the name of Francis Scott Key, sent by President Madison to try to obtain the release of an American physician who was being held captive. He overheard the British plans. They were not going to let him off the ship. As dusk approached he mourned for his fledgling young Nation, and as the sun fell, the bombardment started. Bombs [were] bursting in air. He strained, trying to see, was the flag still there? [He] couldn't see a thing. All night long it continued. At the crack of dawn he ran out to the banister. He looked, straining his eyes, all he could only see [was] dust and debris. '

'Then there was a clearing and he beheld the most beautiful sight he had ever seen – the torn and tattered Stars and Stripes still waving. And many historians say that was the turning point in the War of 1812. We went on to win that war and to retain our freedom. And, if you had gone onto the grounds of Fort McHenry that day, you would

have seen at the base of that flag, the bodies of soldiers who took turns propping up that flag. They would not let that flag go down because they believed in what that flag symbolized. And what did it symbolize? One Nation, under God, indivisible, with liberty and justice for all."[70]

The next day, *The Wall Street Journal* ran an editorial headlined *Ben Carson for President.*[71] Like Ronald Reagan before him, Ben Carson was catapulted into the national political spotlight. In reality, that speech ignited the effort to nominate and elect Ben Carson as the next president of the United States.

Of course, the White House was incensed. And, not surprisingly, in less than three weeks the IRS came knocking on Ben Carson's door. Apparently, the Administration was once again using the power of government to punish its political opponents. But that one speech put Ben Carson on the political map, and perhaps on the road to the White House.

Fortunately, the Obama Administration's clumsy effort to shut up Ben Carson failed. Not surprisingly, the IRS found nothing wrong with Ben Carson's tax filings. Moreover, from every nook and cranny in the nation, men and women, many of whom had never before been engaged in the political process, began calling for Ben Carson to run for president.

Just as Ronald Reagan's communication skills enabled him to speak directly to the American people without the negative filtering of the national news media, Ben Carson has that same power of persuasion and credibility to talk directly to the American people and change the course of history. Some credit Ronald Reagan's power of persuasion for his ability to win the White House in an uphill battle against an incumbent president, Jimmy Carter. Not only did Reagan win in an electoral landslide, but his political coattails were so strong that the Republican Party won control of the United States Senate for the first time since Harry Truman was president.

Being a great communicator is a strong political asset that will not only make Ben Carson a great presidential candidate, but also a great leader. Being able to cast a great vision for our nation and leading it in that direction requires the kind of communications skills that few possess.

As a concrete example of Ben Carson's persuasive abilities and of the high regard in which he is held in the African American community, consider what happened on April 9, 2015 when he spoke at the annual convention of the National Action Network (NAN) that is headed up by Al Sharpton.[72] The presentation of Ben Carson was not announced by Al Sharpton until the morning prior to the afternoon speech. When it was announced there were boos and protests by those attending. But, Al Sharpton told them that they should listen to Ben Carson with respect, and they did.

It is not an exaggeration to say that this was a decidedly hostile audience. In fact, when Al Sharpton spoke from the podium prior to his speech he said that he and Dr. Carson probably did not agree on any issue, and *"I think Dr. Carson and I don't even agree today is Wednesday."*

With that said and an introduction from A.R. Bernard, a political kingmaker in New York City and senior pastor and founder of the Christian Cultural Center megachurch in Brooklyn, who called him *"a leader,"* Ben Carson spoke for nearly 30 minutes. At first the crowd was uneasy, but as Ben Carson laid out his conservative plan for America and related his life story, they warmed to his address. There were no boos, but lots of clapping and cheers for Dr. Carson. And, at the end, according to all reports, people were clamoring to meet him, and several announced on the spot that they were throwing their support behind Ben Carson in his race for the White House.[73]

It is clear that Ben Carson is the only candidate in the race for the Republican nomination for president who could win over an audience like this one. The transformation that occurred at this event provides a crystal clear example of the courage, drawing power, and persuasiveness of Dr. Ben Carson. You should ask yourself what other candidate for president would have attended this event and been able to make a solid conservative case that would be accepted by this audience. This is one of the many reasons that Dr. Ben Carson should be the Republican nominee in 2016.

But, it takes more than the ability to give an inspirational speech to qualify someone to serve as president of the United States. This brings us to the second reason Ben Carson is the best choice for 2016—he will heal and unite our land.

It's no wonder that some Democrat strategists have trouble sleeping at night. If Ben Carson is the 2016 GOP standard bearer, they will not only lose a large share of their black and Hispanic voter base, but also face a man who is a great communicator, and a great leader.

Nominating Ben Carson as the Republican standard bearer in 2016 will give them a case of heartburn from which they may never recover.

Chapter 3
How Ben Carson Will Win

Ben Carson has great respect for Daniel Webster, a famous United States Senator who was known for his forthright integrity and great character. Webster was a powerful orator, a patriot and a statesman. Ben Carson has quoted Daniel Webster on a number of  occasions and respects Webster for his intellect, his education and his wisdom. In fact, Daniel Webster is a good guide for Ben Carson to follow in running for president and overcoming the lie that conservatives are racists and that black conservatives like Carson are traitors to their race. This is Mr. Webster's simple but wise counsel...

> *"There is nothing so powerful as truth, and often nothing so strange."*[74]

Indeed, truth and integrity are the tools that Ben Carson must employ in order to not only win the White House in 2016, but in fact, return our nation to greatness. In addition, this counsel from Jesus to his disciples must also guide Ben Carson...

> *"I'm sending you out like sheep among wolves. So be as cunning as snakes but as innocent as doves."*[75]

Truth, integrity, cunning, and innocence seem to be an unlikely mixture. However, just because Ben Carson has truth on his side, does not mean that he must not be shrewd as he promotes commonsense solutions to

America's problems. Of course, the Democrats' goal is not just to win in 2016, but rather to sweep away all opposition, and establish a permanent Democrat majority. They believe that the current demographic shift will make that possible. If successful, they will abandon the ideals of the Founders and replace them with their own version of socialism, where freedom is limited, economic misery is common, and everyone except the ruling class is equal.

In order to derail the Democrats' plan to dominate the American political process, the false brand that labels all conservatives and Republicans as racist must be overcome and replaced with the truth. After all, it is conservatives and Republicans who are the true friends of all those who seek freedom and success. It is men like Ben Carson who walk in the path of the true historic leadership of the black community. The leadership message of Ben Carson has much more in common with that of Dr. Martin Luther King, Jr., Booker T. Washington, and Frederick Douglass, than does that of Barack Obama, who attended private schools and lived a privileged life.

Ben Carson understands and appreciates the genius of the Founders. The Founders feared big government and especially leaders who ignore the rule of law, which is the foundation of a free society. Patrick Henry might well have been referring to the tendency of president Obama to ignore the Constitution and side step Congress to implement his radical agenda when he said...

"Show me that age and country where the rights and liberties of the people were placed on the sole chance of their rulers being good men, without a consequent loss of liberty."[76]

John Adams was similarly blunt in describing the inevitable result of power being concentrated in the hands of one individual.

"There is danger from all men. The only maxim of a free government ought to be to trust no man living with power to endanger the public liberty."[77]

Henry, Adams and the other Founders understood that to rely on man being good was foolhardy. The Founders suffered under the rule of one man, King George III, and they certainly were not desirous of creating a government under the rule of another man, no matter how good he was. George Washington, praised as the Father of our Country, and once encouraged to set himself up as king, put it succinctly...

"Few men have virtue to withstand the highest bidder."[78]

Those Americans who understand the history of our nation, regardless of their color or ethnic background, understand the danger of powerful centralized government. They justly fear a president who endeavors to run roughshod over the Constitution and the other branches of government. Such a president threatens the liberty of all Americans.

But, although we may agree on the foundational basis of our nation, and on the issues of today, how do conservatives and Republicans rebuild the once strong bond of trust that previously existed between African Americans and other minorities with the GOP?

As we know, it's not a matter of issues. In fact, there is no doubt that the vast majority of minorities share the same hopes and desires as white Americans. They seek, as the Founders put it in the Declaration of Independence... *"Life, liberty, and the pursuit of happiness."* It is the ideas and principles of the Founders that have made the United

States of America the envy of the world and a beacon of hope to millions around the globe. These are timeless ideas, just as important and relevant today as they were when the Founders wrote the Declaration of Independence and authored the United States Constitution.

It is highly doubtful that anyone would choose to live on welfare and be a ward of the state that dictates how you live your life. No one wants to live without hope. That is the most miserable existence that any person can imagine. All hardworking Americans ask is a chance to get a good education, to go as far as they can economically, to raise a family, and to be happy in these pursuits. This is the essence of the Founders' dream.

But, even though the Republican leadership and American conservatives know that their practical and proven approach to government benefits all Americans, especially those mired in poverty, they have failed miserably to establish a beachhead in the African American community, and they have been only slightly more successful in the Latino community.

How does the Republican Party get the truth about their eagerness and their willingness to help all minorities succeed across to African Americans, Hispanics, and Asian Americans? How does it penetrate the fog of lies that all Republicans and conservatives are racists? Truth is our strategy, but what tactics must we employ to not only win one election, but consistently win 30% to 40% of the African America vote and 40% to 60% of the Latin American vote? We live in a high technology era, but it is a low tech approach that may catapult the GOP to its goal.

We already know that nearly 40% of African Americans identify themselves as conservatives and are in sync with conservatives on the important issues of the day.[79] Yet, these same individuals repeatedly vote for Democrats who stand in opposition to what they believe. Why does such a dichotomy between beliefs and voting exist?

The answer is that the black community has only been hearing from one political party, the Democrat Party. They have been very clever in doing so. You see, many, if not most African Americans and Hispanics rely heavily on black and Spanish speaking radio and television programs and stations when it comes to news and entertainment. The reasons for the existence of radio stations, TV networks and programming, as well as magazines and newspapers targeting these two minority groups is somewhat different, but they do provide low cost, high penetration access to these minority groups. Similarly, there are radio stations and newspapers that serve immigrants from Asia. Suffice it to say that in the case of immigrants, the existence of news and entertainment media that serves them is no different than the newspapers written in German, Italian and other languages that served immigrants who arrived on American shores more than 100 years before them.

The existence of such highly targeted news and entertainment mediums provides an opportunity to both parties and to candidates like Ben Carson to reach these audiences directly at a cost much lower than buying time on national radio and television networks. Regrettably, many Republican consultants have, in the past, persuaded the Republican Party and Republican candidates to intentionally not communicate with minority voters. They argued that such communication would only increase the overall voter turnout of these groups and thus increase the Democrat vote total.

The result of following this advice is that for decades the Democrats have been the only party communicating with these groups over the radio stations, television programs, magazines, and newspapers which target this audience. Democrats have used this communications monopoly to not only demonize Republican candidates, but also tell these voters that they are their friends. However, they have not told those voters that they are pro-abortion, favor higher taxes, oppose school vouchers, seek to weaken our military, or have voted to drive up the cost of energy. Meanwhile, the Republican Party and Republican candidates have been silent. They have not responded to the one-sided Democrat attacks.   And, this is the primary reason that African Americans and a growing number of Hispanics vote overwhelmingly for Democrat candidates.

If the only message these minorities hear in election years is from the Democrats, why should we expect the outcome to be any different? The Democrats' communications are so one-sided, of long standing, and without rebuttal, that the Democrats have effectively branded all conservatives and Republicans as racist and xenophobic.

That's why some say winning over substantial numbers of black and Hispanic voters is an impossible task. They argue that the GOP has tried repeatedly to reach minority voters - almost with no success. Actually, the GOP has made little effort, until recently, to reach these voters. Republican efforts typically consist of hiring a black, Hispanic, and Asian outreach coordinator, giving him a small budget and then telling him to reach out to these voters. Almost no funds have been spent to actually reach and win over these voters. It's no wonder the efforts of the GOP have met with limited success.

The good news is that the prevailing advice and wisdom of the Washington, D.C. consultants is wrong. In 2002, extensive baseline testing was conducted to determine if it was possible to reach and persuade black and Hispanic voters to support conservative Republicans running for the United States Senate. This test consisted of radio and television ads directed to these voters over black and Spanish speaking radio and television programs. The results of the test were carefully measured and compared against areas which were not reached by the ads and against results from previous elections where such ads had not been utilized. In other words, all results were baseline tested both horizontally and longitudinally. The results of this test indicated convincingly that winning over black, Hispanic and Asian voters is only a matter of resolve and action. It's not about mimicking the Democrats on the issues, or changing where conservatives stand on the important issues of our day.

Winning the black vote and the Latino vote is not as difficult as some would have us believe. Remember, for 70 years conservative Republicans received 90% or more of the black vote. Yet the Democrats have won a similar share of the African American vote for the past 50 years. So, how does the GOP turn this around? Just highlighting a number of black and Hispanic Republicans at your national convention, mouthing a few platitudes, and appointing a few outreach coordinators is not enough to win over these long disenchanted voters. It will take a sound strategy, straightforward tactics, and money to win back these voters.

Historically, Latinos have voted in large numbers for Republican presidential candidates. In 1980, when Ronald Reagan first ran for president, he won 37% of the Hispanic vote.[80] Twenty-four years later, in 2004, George W. Bush received 44% of the Hispanic vote when he ran for his second term as president.[81]   That's 17% more of the Hispanic vote than Mitt Romney received in 2012.[82]

As an additional indication of the ability of GOP presidential candidates to win over Hispanic voters, consider the results of a poll that found 54% of Hispanics identify themselves as conservative, while only 18% identify themselves as liberal.[83] A significant number of legal Hispanics disapprove of amnesty. After all, they followed the rules and went through the process of becoming citizens. It is also noteworthy that a majority of Latinos who responded to a Univision survey said the border should be secured before there is any discussion of a *"pathway to citizenship"* for illegal immigrants.[84] Why would someone who went through the immigration process legally be supportive of those who broke the law and now want to jump to the front of the line? Instead, they believe these individuals should go through the legal immigration process, just as they did, to become American citizens.

Further evidence of Hispanic support for following the legal process of applying for U.S. Citizenship is the position of the National Hispanic Christian Leadership Conference that represents more than 40,000 Spanish speaking Christian churches in the United States with some 400,000 members. The head of the organization, Samuel Rodriguez, has made it clear that Christians do not condone breaking the law. He said that before illegals are allowed to apply for U.S. citizenship, he would make...

"...illegals go to the back of the line, pay fines, and learn the English language."[85]

And, as for issues like abortion, traditional marriage, taxes, national defense, regulations, job creation, etc., polls show that these Latino Americans are in agreement with conservatives. So, why did they provide overwhelming support to Barack Obama, giving him 71% of the Hispanic vote in 2012?[86]

Unfortunately, the explanation is similar to that for African Americans. While Republicans ignored Hispanic voters or only gave them cursory attention, the Democrats have for years regularly communicated with them over Spanish radio stations and Spanish television networks. The Democrats talked, the Republicans were silent. And, as previously noted, since Hispanics get almost all of their news and opinion from Spanish speaking radio stations and television networks, they heard only one side of the story. And, the side they heard was filled with fabrications and distortions.

The Democrat ads powerfully and deceitfully portrayed Republicans as the enemy of Hispanics. In fact, as you may recall, when Obama addressed an all Hispanic audience, he referred to Republicans as *"our enemies,"* not as the opposition.[87]

In short, these minorities aren't hearing the conservative Republican message supporting policies that create more jobs, lower taxes, provide for a strong national defense and that defend the right-to-life and traditional marriage. It is surprising that they give as much support to Republican candidates as they do.

The solution is for Republicans and Republican candidates to emulate the Democrats' practice of regularly communicating with black and Hispanic voters who agree with them on the issues. The GOP can reach upwardly mobile and Christian African Americans, Hispanic Americans and other minorities over the entertainment and news mediums that they regularly listen to. And, remember, this is not just speculation. This approach has been confirmed through extensive testing over a broad geographic area.

Let's go back to that test that was conducted in 2002 by a firm representing statewide political candidates in five states.[88] They first conducted a survey to identify which blacks and Latinos were conservative in their political outlook. Then, they used this information to determine which radio and TV programs these voters listened to on a regular basis.

They didn't shoot blindly, hoping to reach the targeted groups by buying expensive time on radio and television programs that only a smattering of these minorities were watching. Instead, they wisely used a rifle approach that was much more cost effective.

The radio and television ads they ran were not deceptive. They were clear and straightforward. Moreover, they ran ads that covered the entire spectrum of conservative issues, with an emphasis on social issues such as abortion, educational voucher programs, and traditional marriage. The ads aimed at black conservatives were virtually identical to the ads targeted at Hispanic conservatives. They talked about taxes, jobs, national defense, energy and all the other issues that are important to Americans in general.

After running these ads, they carefully measured the results, comparing how a candidate performed in areas that heard their ads, versus that candidate's performance in areas of similar demographic makeup that did not hear the ads. In addition, they measured their candidate's performance in the targeted area against his performance in that same area in a previous election year (when such targeted ads were not run).

In 19 out of 19 targeted black districts, and 10 out of 10 targeted Hispanic districts, the ads marginally increased the Republican vote.   This was very encouraging. Understandably, when you first tell the truth about the Republicans' stand on an issue, but your brand is that of a racist or xenophobe, it's hard to convince a black or Hispanic voter that you are telling the truth.   This is especially true if the individual candidate did not have previous credibility and standing as a friend and ally of the black and Hispanic voters as does Ben Carson.

The test was quite successful and quite eye opening. But, although it was successful, it was not adopted by the national Republican Party because it was attacked by the Democrats as a voter suppression effort.   Nothing could have been further from the truth.   As you might imagine, winning back the confidence of disenchanted voters is not a quick and easy process.   And, long term success depends on a consistent effort.   In the absence of Ben Carson as the Republican candidate for president in 2016, winning over and solidifying this vote will be a long, drawn out process.

Specifically, here is what the test showed.   A significant number of African Americans (~15%) and Hispanics (~32%) thought twice about voting for the Democrat candidate.   This segment of voters did not trust the Republican candidate enough to vote for him.   But, the ads by the Republican candidates exposed the reality that the Republican Party and conservatives have more in common with their views than do the Democrats.   But this non-voting group had neither the necessary trust to vote for a Republican nor the necessary trust in the Democrat candidate to vote for either candidate.

Considering that this was a one-time test that was not followed up in subsequent elections, it was a great success.

In fact, the change in voting by African Americans and Hispanics altered the outcome of several of these close-run statewide elections.

Moreover, the worst fears of the Washington, D.C. consultants were not realized. Instead, the Republican candidates received more votes from African Americans and Hispanic Americans and the Democrats received less because fewer blacks and Latinos actually voted. These disaffected voters were in that middle ground, transition stage. They agreed with the Republican candidate on the issue, but did not yet trust him.

But, that's not really the point. In these tests, a typical Republican candidate received about 12% of the black vote and about 33% of the Hispanic vote. Had the Republican Party ignored the advice of the Republican consultants decades ago and made it a regular practice to run such ads in every election, their vote total would never have plummeted to the degree it did in 2012. Instead, 35 to 40 percent of the black vote and 50 to 60 percent of the Hispanic vote would have eventually made their way across the aisle to vote regularly for conservative Republican candidates.

Again, this is a process. It's not about winning one election or about just winning 12% to 15% of the black vote. It's about regularly winning at least 37% of the African American vote (the percent of African Americans who identify themselves as conservative) and at least 54% of the Hispanic vote (the percent of Hispanics that identify themselves as conservative). That is the objective, and achieving this goal can happen if the Republican Party takes the necessary steps to reach those goals.

Better yet, by nominating Ben Carson as the Republican standard bearer in 2016, the GOP can leap forward to those goals immediately. The nomination of Ben Carson provides an amazing opportunity for the Republican Party. Just imagine what will happen if the Republican nominee for president in 2016 is Dr. Benjamin Carson. Instead of taking 20 or 30 years to regain the support of black and Latino Americans, the Republican Party will reclaim a large share of the black and Hispanic vote in just one election. The nomination of Ben Carson will have the political impact of the election of Franklin D. Roosevelt in 1932. It can be a turning point, a demarcation line. It can put the Democrat Party on defense for decades to come.

There is every reason to believe that Ben Carson will win 35 to 40 percent of the black vote and 45 to 50 percent of the Hispanic vote. Such numbers guarantee that Ben Carson will almost certainly win the White House by a wide margin. Remember, a Republican candidate for president only needs to win 17% of the black vote to create a roadblock to Hillary winning the White House in 2016. Perhaps even more important, Ben Carson would set the Republican Party firmly on the path to regularly winning a large share of support from minority voters, no matter who future nominees are, providing they are conservative.

Remember, the impact of running ads directly to black and Hispanics was tested in 2014 with great success. Thom Tillis is a United States Senator today because the National Draft Ben Carson for President Committee spent more than $300,000 on radio ads over black and Spanish speaking radio stations in North Carolina. Those ads proved that just the name of Ben Carson has great sway with African American and Hispanic voters.

By personally campaigning in black and Hispanic areas, presidential candidate Carson will challenge the Democrats on their home turf. By speaking in black churches, and quite possibly receiving the support of black leaders and entertainers, Ben Carson will usher in a new era in American politics.

Through radio, television, newspaper and magazine advertising, as well as personal appearances, presidential candidate Ben Carson will put the Democrats on notice that they can no longer count on blacks and Hispanics voting en masse for them. By matching the Democrat nominee's advertising budget to these groups dollar-for-dollar, Ben Carson will win the White House and change history. Equally important, the Democrat nominee will be forced to debate the issues rather than just smear the Republican presidential candidate as being a racist, or in the case of Ben Carson, an *Uncle Tom.*

Hillary Clinton (or whoever the Democrat nominee is) will have to explain why she supports the right of a woman to abort a baby right until the minute before it is born. She will have to explain why she cares more about supporting the teachers union than about helping black and Latino students by implementing voucher programs. She will have to provide an explanation as to why she opposes the traditional definition of marriage as being between a man and a woman. And, why she would appoint judges who attack a Christian's right of free speech in the public square. She will have to explain why she is for higher taxes that kill jobs, and why she favors a weaker national defense that puts America at risk. And, she will have to explain why she is against commonsense efforts to reduce energy prices and why she wants to engage in sweetheart green energy deals that benefit crony capitalists and hurt consumers, especially the poor.

And, just suppose that presidential candidate Ben Carson picks New Mexico Governor Susana Martinez as his vice-presidential running mate. Carson and Martinez would make huge inroads into the African American and Hispanic communities without compromising their conservative ideals and values one iota. It would be the Republicans that are on attack, and the Democrats that are forced into being on the defensive. It's hard to make the case that the Republicans are waging a war on women and on minorities when their ticket is composed of a man, a woman, an African American and a Hispanic.

This is not to suggest that Ben Carson should not contest strongly for the white vote, especially the independent voters. He should, and he will. There is no logical reason whatsoever to assume that Ben Carson would be any less successful than any other Republican candidate for president in winning at least 60% of the white vote. Facing such a situation, there would be no path to victory for Hillary Clinton or for Joe Biden or Elizabeth Warren.

Just imagine, for a moment, if you will, a debate between Ben Carson and Hillary Clinton. Don't get me wrong, Hillary is an intelligent and highly educated person. She's a tough campaigner, but up against Dr. Ben Carson, she will meet her match and more. Hillary has political experience on her side. Ben Carson has truth on his side. In order to be successful as a medical innovator, he has had to debate some of the smartest physicians in the world, the kind of men who pull no punches when arguing for or against a new procedure advocated by Dr. Carson. Ben Carson may speak softly, but he is a tough and experienced debater who speaks with courage and integrity.

As the Republican nominee Ben Carson will shatter the lie that all Republicans and conservatives are racists. He will derail and dismantle the Democrats' plan to create a permanent Democrat majority. And, as a successful president who unleashes the power of the free market and lifts millions out of poverty, the Democrats' dreams of turning the United States of America into a socialist state will be demolished. Once the lie that Republicans and conservatives are racist is buried, the stage would be set for conservative candidates to win a majority of the black and Hispanic vote in the years and decades ahead, and to unite our nation as one people dedicated to the United States Constitution, and to the preservation of our republic as the last best hope of freedom on the globe.

When you consider that the Republican Party is the historic home of emigrants and African Americans, it should not be too hard to envision the day when Hispanics, Asians, and black Americans rally to the banner of the GOP. It can happen on Election Day 2016, if the GOP has the wisdom to nominate Ben Carson as their candidate for president.

But again, just being black is not enough. Just being Hispanic is not enough. Just being Asian is not enough. It will take someone like Dr. Ben Carson, who is held in high regard in the black community, the Hispanic community, and in the Asian community to once and for all time demolish the lie that Republicans and conservatives are racist. Dr. Carson and his wife, Candy, have a track record of compassion, caring, and involvement in the lives of aspiring Americans of all races and all nationalities. Ben Carson has a personal understanding of the plight of growing up in poverty. He knows how hard it is to escape poverty. He knows that the key to economic success is a quality education, good character, hard work and perseverance.

By choosing Ben Carson as the Republican candidate for president in 2016, and by making an all-out effort to reach black and Hispanic voters, the Republicans can not only win in 2016, but also in subsequent presidential and congressional elections.

Make no mistake about it, nominating and electing Ben Carson will take tens of millions, even hundreds of millions of dollars, but it is the only clear path to victory in 2016. Continuing to follow the bad advice of the Washington, D.C. political operatives who suggest that the Republican Party and conservatives should continue to ignore black and Hispanic voters is the sure path to defeat. The Democrats may have lost in 2010 and 2014, but they won the White House handily in 2008, and again in 2012. Make no mistake about it, they expect to win the White House again in 2016. They believe the demographics are in their favor, that they have an edge in technology and organization, and that the Republican nominee will be unable to make significant inroads into winning over minority voters.

The worst course of action for the Republican Party would be to nominate a candidate who moves to the left and ignores the social issues that are so important to a large segment of Hispanic, black and Asian voters. Such a nominee will keep the Republicans on the outside looking in. And that would spell dire consequences for our nation.

The 2016 Republican presidential nominee must support traditional values like marriage between a man and a woman, must oppose abortion, must support a return to prayer in schools, favor lower taxes, a strong national defense, school choice, and insist on border security. He must have a plan, like Ben Carson, to repeal and replace Obamacare with a free market program that doesn't violate the patient-doctor relationship. These are the issues on which there is common ground with large numbers of voters in the African American and Hispanic communities.

Ben Carson is a sure bet to not only win the White House, but also heal our broken land, as the next chapter explains.

Chapter 4
Ben Carson Will Heal Our Broken Land

Abraham Lincoln's second inaugural address was not what his listeners or the American people, North and South, expected. They expected a victory speech. The end was near for the South. The war was finally going well for the North. Thus,  Lincoln's listeners expected Lincoln to trumpet his success in conquering the South. They expected him to boast of his victory and to explain how he was going to punish the South. They wanted a war dance and revenge. Instead, Lincoln spoke words of reconciliation.

Lincoln saw his first responsibility was to win the war and preserve the American republic. He didn't seek punishment or revenge. Instead he sought peace, reconciliation and harmony. Lincoln said in part...

> *"Fondly do we hope, fervently do we pray, that this mighty scourge of war may speedily pass away. Yet, if God wills that it continue until all the wealth piled by the bondsman's two hundred and fifty years of unrequited toil shall be sunk, and until every drop of blood drawn with the lash shall be paid by another drawn with the sword, as was said three thousand years ago, so still it must be said 'the judgments of the Lord are true and righteous altogether.'*
> *With malice toward none, with charity for all, with firmness in the right as God gives us to see the right, let us strive on to finish the work we are in, to bind up the nation's wounds, to care for him*

*who shall have borne the battle and for his widow
and his orphan, to do all which may achieve and
cherish a just and lasting peace among ourselves
and with all nations."*[89]

Lincoln sought reconciliation and harmony, while many
in the North sought revenge and retribution. While Lincoln
was unwilling to compromise the freedom won for African
Americans, he wanted to heal the nation, and reconcile
Southerner to Northerner and black to white. He was firm
in his commitment to not only freeing the slaves, but also to
their welfare and to their full rights as American citizens.

In Lincoln's last public speech before he was
assassinated, he expressed support for the voting
enfranchisement of recently freed black Americans.[90] Upon
hearing Lincoln's words, John Wilkes Booth, who was in
the audience, was overheard to say, *"This is the last speech
he will ever make."*[91] Indeed, just three days later, Booth, a
white supremacist Democrat, killed President Abraham
Lincoln. Not only was Lincoln's dream of reconciliation set
back a hundred years, so was his determination to grant the
full rights of citizenship to African Americans.

Today, nearly 150 years after Lincoln's Second
Inaugural Address, America is nearly as divided as it was
when Lincoln spoke in 1865. In fact, a recent poll indicates
that the issue of race relations has once again risen to
become the top concern of many Americans.[92] Sadly, this
disunity and disharmony have been encouraged by
President Obama and United States Attorney General Eric
Holder. Moreover, it is highly unlikely that this effort will
abate prior to the end of President Obama's term in office.
In fact, should Hillary Clinton, Elizabeth Warren, Joe Biden
or any other Democrat be elected president in 2016, such
efforts are sure to continue. In fact, as previously noted,

the encouragement of racial division is a political strategy deeply embedded in the Democrat Party. But such a strategy threatens the very survival of our nation. As Abraham Lincoln said in a speech after being nominated to run for the United States Senate in 1858...

"A house divided against itself cannot stand."[93]

When President Obama, Hillary Clinton, Elizabeth Warren, Joe Biden et al. encourage anger, jealousy, distrust and even hatred between Americans, they fail in their first task of leadership: American unity. Without unity, America is weak and vulnerable to the advances of our enemies around the globe. Without unity, America and Americans suffer. There is no advance without unity, there is no progress without unity, and there is no strength without unity.

One of the first challenges of our next president will be to restore American unity and harmony. This does not mean sweeping problems under the rug, but it does mean emphasizing the fact that the things that unite us as Americans are far greater and more important than the things about which we disagree. It means providing a vision of the future that is better for all Americans without any regard whatsoever to their nation of origin, their race, their sex, their age or their economic status. It means unifying Americans to face challenges that threaten the entire nation and persuading them to coalesce behind commonsense solutions to our nation's most pressing problems. And it means reminding Americans of the foundational principles of our nation, our rich heritage of freedom, our many accomplishments, and our record of triumph in the face of danger or against seemingly insurmountable odds.

Let's be honest. No other potential candidate for President of the United States on the Republican ticket is in a position to bring unity and harmony to our land as is Dr.

Benjamin Solomon Carson. Yes, perhaps another candidate could squeak out a victory, but it would not be a victory of unity and harmony. America would remain a divided nation, a situation sure to be exacerbated by those in our society who wish to tear down our nation, not build it up.

Ben Carson is the one principled conservative running for President in 2016 who has the ability to reach out to all Americans, whether they are white, black, or have their roots in Mexico, Venezuela, Bolivia, Guatemala, Ecuador, China, India, Philippines or any other nation. It is because of Ben Carson's personal story of overcoming poverty and achieving success and, yes, the color of his skin, that every American of goodwill will listen to him just as they were open to hearing and supporting Barack Obama. Americans of all races and nationalities are anxious to put this dangerous divide behind us, but it will take a man such as Ben Carson to accomplish that feat. As a Christian, Ben Carson understands that in the absence of justice, contrition, repentance and forgiveness, no healing of society can occur. No progress will be made in bringing harmony and unity to our land. Revenge, envy, jealousy destroy healing and unity. Leadership and policies driven by such attitudes only exacerbate disharmony and divide our nation.

Ben Carson earned the trust and the respect of men and women of all races and backgrounds *before* he ever entered the political arena. It is the existence of this trust that existed for many decades that uniquely places him in a position to heal and unite our nation. It is Dr. Carson's character that has made him one of the most respected men in America by men and women of all races and backgrounds.

As an example of Dr. Carson's character and colorblind approach to others, consider his outlook for those he served as a neurosurgeon...

"I was doing an interview on NPR and I was asked, 'Why don't you talk about race very often?' And I said it's because I'm a neurosurgeon -- and I got a very quizzical look. And I said, 'You see, when I take someone to the operating room, and I shave their head, and I open the scalp and take off bone flap, and open the dura, I am then operating on the thing that makes that person who they are. The skin has very little [to do] with who that person is. And it's something that we have just allowed to define us and it really has very little to do with who a person is."[94]

Dr. Benjamin Solomon Carson is uniquely gifted, positioned and qualified to unite and lead our nation during these perilous times. Bringing America together again is one of the reasons that Ben Carson is running for president. Our Pledge of Allegiance is more than just words to Ben Carson, it is what he believes our nation must be, *"...one nation, under God, with liberty and justice for all."*

For his entire life, Ben Carson has been a healer, someone who comforts patients in distress, someone who brings people together, someone who is trusted to work for the good of all. After all, healing is what the medical profession is all about.

But more than that, American unity is the historic hallmark of our nation. In fact, the words *E Pluribus Unum* are found on the Great Seal of the United States and on all of our coins. Those Latin words translate as *"out of many one."* This was made the motto of the United States by the Continental Congress in 1782 and it remained the motto of the United States until 1956 when it was replaced by the words *"In God We Trust."* Nevertheless, the words *E Pluribus Unum* still signify a powerful and uniquely American concept. Initially, they referred to the creation of the United States out of the thirteen colonies. More generally, they have been understood to also convey the creation of the United States out of immigrants from many lands. In other words, even though people emigrated here from every nation on the globe, and even though they have different customs and different traditions, we are all Americans, we are one people.

This concept is unique to the United States. If a Frenchman immigrates to India and becomes a citizen of India, he will never be regarded as an Indian. Similarly, if an Englishman immigrates to China and becomes a Chinese citizen, he will never become Chinese. It is only when one immigrates to America that he becomes *"an American."* Dinesh D'Souza puts it this way...

> *"America is not defined by blood or birth but by the adoption of the nation's Constitution, its laws, and its shared way of life. That's how the Irish, the Italians, and the Jews, and today the Koreans, the South Asians, and the West Indians, can all come to this country and in time 'become American.'"*[95]

It is not only a wonderful concept, but one that is critical to America moving forward in the 21st century. Regardless of our lineage, we have all assimilated into being Americans, not Irish Americans or German Americans or Mexican Americans—just Americans. This assimilation and unity is the strength of our nation. While we are a diverse nation of many talents and unique characteristics, it is not our diversity that makes us strong, it is our unity that makes us impregnable as a nation. And, that is the reason the title of Ben Carson's book is just that, *"One Nation."*

Unity was the theme of the founding of our republic. Without unity we could not have won our independence in the American Revolution. It was the ideal of the Founders. It is the theme of Ben Carson's presidential campaign.

For Ben Carson, American unity and comity is not just a nice idea or an ideal goal; it is absolutely vital to the survival and resurgence of our nation. Without American unity that is built upon the founding principles of this nation, we will never again be the great and good nation that has defended freedom around the globe, and has generously come to the aid of others for nearly 240 years. The torch on the top of the Statue of Liberty figuratively and literally represents the United States as the beacon of freedom and justice to the world. Lady Liberty's torch has welcomed millions from around the globe to not only be citizens of the United States, but, more importantly, Americans.

In 2004, a handsome young state senator from Illinois gave the keynote address at the Democrat National Convention.[96] The speech Barack Obama gave that night was hopeful and optimistic. He referred to America as a *"magical place"* and as a *"beacon of freedom and opportunity"* to the world. He said that his parents gave him the name Barack, which means *"blessed"* because they believed that in America your name is no obstacle to success. And, he pointed out that in America, *"...you don't have to be rich to achieve your potential."*

Barack Obama said, *"I stand here knowing that my story is part of the larger American story, that I owe a debt to all of those who came before me, and that in no other country on Earth is my story even possible."*[97]

He continued, *"Tonight, we gather to affirm the greatness of our nation not because of the height of our skyscrapers, or the power of our military, or the size of our economy; our pride is based on a very simple premise, summed up in a Declaration made over two hundred years ago: 'We hold these truths to be self-evident, that all men are created*

*equal... that they are endowed by their Creator
with certain inalienable rights, that among these
are life, liberty and the pursuit of happiness."*[98]

And, in his 2008 victory speech, President-Elect
Barack Obama stated, *"In this country, we rise or fall as
one nation, as one people."*[99]

This statement lent hope to the idea that America was
finally entering a post-racial society, one where race and
color did not matter, where the dream of Dr. Martin Luther
King, Jr. would finally be realized that American...

*"....children will one day live in a nation where they
will not be judged by the color of their skin, but by
the content of their character."*[100]

The speeches of Barack Obama were not only stirring
and moving, they implied a desire for unity and harmony
and they praised the greatness of America. But, sadly, they
were apparently just words. With the election of Barack
Obama, we were promised the advent of a post-racial society
and a new era of harmony and racial reconciliation. Instead,
what we received was a president and an attorney general
who have, whether intentionally or unintentionally, divided
Americans on the basis of race and any other difference that
would create disunity. Instead of racial harmony, we have
experienced the worst and most offensive efforts to divide
the races. No effort has been made by the Obama White
House and no effort will be made by a Hillary Clinton White
House or an Elizabeth Warren White House to bring
America together. If we elect Clinton, or Warren, or Biden
or any other Democrat, we can expect four or eight more
years of efforts to inflame racial division between white and
black Americans.

The fact is that President Obama, Hillary Clinton,
Elizabeth Warren, Joe Biden and the Democrat Party in
general, reject the vision of the United States of America as a

good, great and generous nation. They see the United States as neither good, nor great, nor generous. In fact, they see America as the source of almost all the problems in the world. So instead of wisely following the principles of America's Founders, they seek a top down government where they, the self-identified *"enlightened,"* rule over the citizens of this land. Why? Because they believe they know better how we should live, how we should think and how we should act, than we do. In fact, they believe that they are ethically superior to those they wish to rule over. They don't believe in American unity and assimilation under the ideals of the Founders, they believe in diversity, and, as Obama said in *"fundamentally transforming America."*[101] By transformation, they mean to undue the principles of the Founders and replace them with their dream of a socialist utopia. Consistent with their embrace of Saul Alinsky, who dedicated his book to Lucifer, Obama and Clinton have been seduced by the original sin in the Garden of Eden, wanting to be like God, to wield power over others.[102]

These new Democrats are utopians. Instead of understanding that every nation makes mistakes because men are imperfect, they seek an ideal that has its roots in the French Revolution. They reject the idea of Godly wisdom, and instead seek to replace it with human reason.

And, because they are convinced that their cause is right and just, they believe the ends justify the means. Apparently, that's why they have intentionally set Americans against each other. They have encouraged anger and jealousy by workers against employers. They have promoted division between men and women and between younger Americans and older Americans. Instead of encouraging success, they seek to create rage against the successful, by those trapped in poverty (ironically by their own policies). They wish to punish achievement, and make our nation repent and suffer for the wrongs they believe it has done.   And, perhaps most destructive of all, they have set one race or ethnic group against another solely for political gain.

Their plan of action is to divide and conquer, so that they can live as princes and potentates, while those they rule over suffer.   Theirs is the path to tyranny.   But, President Ben Carson will call upon the American people to reject the twin evils of jealously and envy.   As president he will set a tone of civility, respect for the law and equal justice under the law.   He will accord his opponents the respect they deny him.   However, Ben Carson will never abandon the principles of the Founders or initiate policies detrimental to the United States for political gain.

In stark contrast, President Benjamin Carson will emphasize and promote the things that unify us as Americans: love of country, faith in God, belief in fairness, a desire for justice, common decency, civil discourse, generosity, courage and opportunity for all.   By his own example, President Carson will lead America up from the valley of envy and jealously, to the mountain top of harmony and goodwill.   There is nothing that better personifies the vision of Ben Carson than a desire that Americans work together, live together and succeed together in peaceful accord. Ben Carson is a man of his word.

Ben Carson's moral leadership and emphasis on the importance of good character and hard work will provide inspiration and healing to all Americans.   His campaign and his Administration will signal the coming together of America, united by common goals and common aspirations.   Like Ronald Reagan's theme, morning in America, Ben Carson's message is one of goodwill and hope for all Americans.

Chapter 5
Ben Carson: Trustworthy Conservative

Beyond skill and knowledge, what is the one thing that you need most in a doctor? It is trustworthiness. Just as fidelity and mutual trust are the twin foundations of a lasting marriage, a man running for public office must be someone who will be faithful to the words he speaks and the commitments he makes. Mouthing conservative positions and then abandoning them after being elected is something politicians too often do. Equally frustrating is someone who touts his conservative stands and then proceeds to wallow in pork barrel spending and support subsidies that hurt consumers by reducing competition. No, what America needs today is Ben Carson, a man who will not be dissuaded from pursuing what is best for America because politics or political obligations get in his way. He is a man who can be trusted to abide by the spirit and the letter of the United States Constitution.

When Jesus spoke to the crowds about John the baptizer, he asked them,

"What did you go into the desert to see? Tall grass swaying in the wind?"[103]

In other words, were they looking for someone who would simply change what he was saying according to the way the wind was blowing? As the forerunner of Jesus, John spoke the truth. If he did not do so, his words would have been meaningless.

Similarly, a politician's words are meaningless if he is not faithful to them. Sadly, too many politicians, both Republican and Democrat, are simply *"grass swaying in the wind.*"[104]   They say one thing and then they do something entirely opposite when they are elected. Too often both Republicans and Democrats are a part of the problem. Neither party is completely trustworthy.

Some of those in public office have good intentions and sound principles. Unfortunately, their intentions and principles are not matched by their actions. Their character fails them when push comes to shove. It's easy to espouse high principles; it's much more difficult to live by them.

Ben Carson is a mortal, flawed man, just like you and me. But, throughout the crucible of life he has proven himself to be a man of humility and character. And, since he has entered the political arena, he has shown both courage and wisdom.

Can you think of another man who would have had the courage to speak so boldly to the president of the United States, telling him that his signature accomplishment, the Affordable Care Act, aka Obamacare, was a disaster?[105] In fact, Dr. Carson's entire life has been exemplified by courage and honesty in the face of strong opposition. On a number of occasions he sought to use an innovative new procedure to try and save a life that others had given up on. But, when he wanted to do so, he faced strong opposition from doctors who disagreed with his approach. Accordingly, Ben Carson was forced to defend and debate those doctors who disagreed with his approach. And, because such debates deal with life and death matters, the doctors involved engage in no-holds-barred debates, but never in personalities or emotions.

In fact, Ben Carson's medical colleagues gave him the nickname *"longshot"* because of his willingness to try new procedures on seemingly hopeless cases.[106] In fact, on more than one occasion, he was advised that if he proceeded he would risk his reputation. But, Ben Carson, unlike a number of doctors and almost every politician, wasn't concerned about his reputation; he was only concerned about the lives of those who he treated. He put their life before any potential damage to himself.

It was more than that, however. Ben Carson has written a book titled "*Take the Risk*," that outlines a clear best/worst case risk analysis process that he follows when making important medical and personal decisions.[107] It is hard to imagine another candidate for president who has so much experience in making tough decisions under such extreme pressure. Few, if any, governors or senators have had to make instant life and death decisions.

As noted, Ben Carson's risk analysis procedure is not based primarily on how it affects him, but rather on how it affects others. In his book he provides numerous examples of how this analysis has kept him on track, both in his personal life, as well as in his professional career. It is a simple and straightforward approach...

- ✶ What is the best thing that can happen if I do this?
- ✶ What is the worst thing that can happen if I do this?
- ✶ What is the best thing that can happen if I don't do it?
- ✶ What is the worst thing that can happen if I don't do it?[108]

Perhaps the most important point he makes in the entire book is captured in this one sentence...

"I would reemphasize, however, another favorite point: that wisdom is different from, and often more critical than, knowledge."[109]

While Hillary Clinton and Elizabeth Warren rely on intelligence and human reason, Ben Carson adds an even more important ingredient, Godly wisdom. In a similar vein, Ben Carson has written that...

> *"Many people use the terms wisdom and knowledge interchangeably. They are, however, quite different, and having one in no way confers the other. Knowledge is familiarity with facts. The more knowledge one has, the more things one is capable of doing, but only with wisdom is one able to discern which of the many things they are capable of doing should be pursued and in what order."*[110]

Dr. Carson clearly understands the importance of wisdom, not just knowledge and intelligence, in making decisions that affect the lives of millions of Americans. In other words, Ben Carson relies on Godly wisdom just as the Founders did. Accordingly, when it comes to issues, his perspective is in alignment with the Founders. He understands the importance of the rule of law, of limiting the power of government, of the division of powers, of financial responsibility, and the importance of the federal system of government.

Historian Paul Kengor has identified eleven principles of what he calls a *"Reagan Conservative."*[111] They are...

* Freedom
* Faith
* Family
* Sanctity and dignity of human life
* American exceptionalism
* The Founders' wisdom and vision
* Lower taxes
* Limited government
* Peace through strength
* Anti-communism
* Belief in the individual

Although anti-communism might not come high on a list today, it is evident that this evil ideology is not dead. In North Korea, China, Vietnam, Cuba, Venezuela, Nicaragua and at other outposts around the globe, including Russia, communism is not dead, it is resurgent. However, if Reagan were to write out a list today, he would probably simply list his focus as Islamic fascism and other forms of aggressive totalitarianism, including communism.

That one entry on the list aside, this list, as compiled by Professor Kengor, seems to well define a Ronald Reagan conservative. Importantly, Kengor points out that each one of these principles is intertwined. For instance, Ronald Reagan wasn't for lower taxes as something that works and is fair, but more important to Reagan was the fact that lower taxes means more freedom for the individual because he is able to spend or invest the fruits of his own labors. In other words, lower taxes were an issue of freedom in Ronald Reagan's mind. In fact, in Ronald Reagan's first appearance on the national political stage, the theme of his *"A Time for Choosing"* speech was about freedom. And, of course, that freedom depended on winning the cold war by following a policy of peace through strength, and shrinking the size of government. Accordingly, limiting the size and power of government was in keeping with the Founders' vision of a limited government.

Even intellectuals on the left like Hillary Clinton and Elizabeth Warren insist that they are champions of freedom, but they reject the link between faith and freedom. However, as Ronald Reagan pointed out...

"Learning is a good thing, but unless it's tempered by faith and a love of freedom, it can be very dangerous indeed. The names of many intellectuals are recorded on the rolls of infamy,

from Robespierre to Lenin to Ho Chi Minh to Pol Pot."[112]

Ronald Reagan remains not only the touchstone of the Republican Party, but also the last universally acknowledged great president by a vast majority of Americans. Of course, as noted earlier, no one can rightfully claim the mantle of Ronald Reagan, yet I can think of no other Republican candidate for president who more closely personifies the principles, the character, the optimism and the sunny disposition of Ronald Reagan than Dr. Benjamin Carson.

In keeping with his humble approach to life, Ben Carson has never lusted after the office of president. To the contrary, he chose to run only after more than five hundred thousand Americans called on him to run through their clamorings and petitions. Even then, he was reluctant to run until he felt that God was calling him to serve. It is not something he has undertaken lightly, yet it is now something that he is totally committed to.

His motivation to run for president is something he is doing because he feels the United States of America is in danger of falling from its pinnacle position in the world and is on its descent to becoming just another nation. He fears that the beacon of freedom and hope that the United States represents to the world is being snuffed out. He fears that his children, and successive generations of children, will not live in a land of hope and opportunity, but rather be relegated to live in a country where the government and its many bureaucrats and politicians reign supreme, while the people languish in socialism.

With no axe to grind, no personal ambition to fulfill, Dr. Ben Carson is the one conservative running for president you can trust to be faithful to the principles of freedom, and to protect and defend the United States of America from enemies foreign and domestic.

Ben Carson is the right choice for 2016 not just because he is sure to win, sure to heal and can be trusted to follow the United States Constitution. He is also the right choice because he is blessed with the right leadership skills and experience to lead our nation in this time of great crisis. Ben Carson is not a professional, career politician and, frankly, the last thing this nation needs at this critical juncture is another career politician. In fact, Ben Carson is exactly the kind of man the Founders envisioned serving in public office as the leader of this nation. They didn't want politics to be a career. They wanted men for whom it would be a sacrifice to take a few years out of their life to serve in public office. They envisioned men of talent, ability, and achievement, like Dr. Ben Carson, to serve as congressmen, senators and as president of the United States. In fact, as we shall see, one of America's greatest presidents, a man who saved our republic, had much less experience than does Ben Carson.

Chapter 6
Ben Carson: Prepared to Serve

When former U.S. Attorney General Edwin Meese was asked how Ronald Reagan, an actor who had never before held public office, could become an effective governor and a great president, he said that the key to Ronald Reagan's success was four strengths...[113]

1. **Principles.** Ronald Reagan had firm principles of governance that guided him in all decisions.
2. **Vision.** Ronald Reagan had a clear vision of where he wanted to take the nation.
3. **People.** Ronald Reagan understood people. He knew how to work with them to accomplish his objectives.
4. **Persuasion.** Ronald Reagan had the ability to bring together men with different points of view, as well as millions of Americans, and persuade them to follow him.

General Meese said that Ronald Reagan had been a leader early in his life. He was elected student body president at his high school, senior class president at his college, and he became an officer in the Army shortly after leaving college.

Similarly, Ben Carson has a lifelong history of leadership and executive experience. As mentioned previously, he was named corps commander of all ROTC units in the City of Detroit in just three years. And, because he set a record on the ROTC examination for officer, Carson was offered a commission to West Point. Similarly, in 1984, at just 33 years of age, he was named the youngest major division head of Johns Hopkins University Hospital in its more than one hundred year history.

Ben Carson not only ran a multi-hundred million dollar division at Johns Hopkins University Hospital, he also started and served as CEO of a nonprofit that operates in all fifty states. In addition, he has served for nearly two decades on the board of two multi-billion dollar corporations—Costco and the Kellogg Company.

As noted in the previous chapter, Ben Carson has been forced to make life and death decisions quickly, and under tremendous pressure. This is the kind of experience few have before becoming president, yet the ability to make the right decision under extreme stress is critical to success and to the security of the United States.

General Meese said that one of the most important attributes of Ronald Reagan was his character. He observed that President Reagan was a humble man, even as president. He was honest and straightforward. Clearly, in the mind of General Meese, character is one of the most important, if not the most important, attributes of a great president.

While former U.S. Attorney General Meese has not endorsed the presidential candidacy of Ben Carson, he made it clear that he greatly admires him as a man of character.

The life and career of Ben Carson have many parallels with that of Ronald Reagan. Both were born poor. Both benefitted greatly from having a Godly mother. Reagan was and Carson has been a leader since a young age.

Like Reagan, Ben Carson is a humble man of good character. A good illustration of his humility and his character is the story of what happened to him when he was a young doctor at Johns Hopkins. Here is that story in Carson's own words...

"...when I was an intern at Johns Hopkins back in 1977, the sight of a black physician was decidedly rare. Often when I would go onto a hospital ward while wearing my surgical scrubs, a nurse would say, 'I'm sorry, but Mr. Patient is not quite ready to be taken to the operating room yet,' assuming that I was an orderly. After many years of hard work to achieve the title of doctor, many might say that I would have been justified in reacting angrily to the suggestion that I was an orderly, especially given the racial overtones of the misunderstanding. However, I tried to look at things from the nurse's perspective. The only black males she had seen come onto that ward wearing surgical scrubs were orderlies who were coming to pick up or deliver a patient. Why would she think differently in my case? A highly sensitive individual would have created a scene and everyone would have felt uncomfortable. I would simply say in those situations, 'I'm sorry that Mr. Patient isn't ready yet, but I'm Dr. Carson and I'm here for another reason.'"

"The offending nurse would often be so embarrassed that I actually felt sorry for her or him and would say, 'It's quite all right and you don't need to feel bad.' I would be very nice to that person, and I would have another friend for life."[114]

As you can see, Dr. Ben Carson shares the four strengths that Ed Meese identified as the key to Ronald Reagan's success as governor and as president...

1. **Principles.** Ben Carson firmly believes in the Founders' principles of a limited government, a strong national defense, a sound financial foundation and traditional values.

2. **Vision.** Ben Carson's vision is clear. He will return America to fiscal sanity, replace Obamacare

with health savings accounts, lower taxes, end class warfare, eschew political correctness, rebuild our military and re-establish respect for America around the globe.

3. **People.** Ben Carson, like Reagan, understands people. He recognizes their strengths and their shortcomings. He knows how to inspire and lead.

4. **Persuasion.** Ben Carson is blessed with the ability to persuade differing parties to reach solutions that are in the best interest of the United States of America. His power of persuasion will not only enable him to lead our nation in the right direction, but also help to heal and unify our nation.

But, just as the Republican establishment did not immediately embrace Ronald Reagan, it is slow to embrace Ben Carson. Ben's not a member of the *"club"* even though he played a valuable role in electing a Republican majority to the U.S. Senate in 2014.

Truthfully, it will take an outsider, a non-politician such as Ben Carson to get our nation back on track, just like it took Ronald Reagan, another Washington, D.C. outsider, to restore freedom and prosperity to our land.

Of course, Ben Carson's detractors say that Ben Carson is a nice fellow, an outstanding doctor, articulate and right on the issues, but they're not sure he's ready to be president. They are concerned that he is not a politician and has never been elected to public office. Of course, virtually all of these comments come from politicians.

As far as having previously been elected to public office is concerned, his detractors are right, he has not been elected to public office, and thank goodness. All of our current problems have been created by career politicians from both political parties. The United States doesn't need more *"inside the beltway"* political experience in its next president; it needs a man blessed with great insight, common sense, calm strength and Godly wisdom. America needs a strong leader, a man of character, a president with a clear vision and someone with experience in making hard decisions under pressure.

Perhaps it is not an accident that Ben Carson's middle name is Solomon. Solomon, at less than 20 years of age, with no experience whatsoever, became the King of Israel. Yet, Solomon was the greatest leader of the world as it existed at that time. Why was Solomon so successful? The explanation is provided in the Bible...

"In Gibeon the Lord appeared to Solomon in a dream at night. He said, 'What can I give you?' Solomon responded, 'You've shown great love to my father David, who was your servant. He lived in your presence with truth, righteousness, and commitment. And you continued to show him your great love by giving him a son to sit on his throne today. Lord my God, although I'm young and inexperienced, you've made me king in place of my father David. I'm among your people whom you have chosen. They are too numerous to count or record. Give me a heart that listens so that I can judge your people and tell the difference between good and evil. After all, who can judge this great people of yours? The Lord was pleased that Solomon asked for this. God replied, 'You've asked for this and not for long life, or riches for yourself, or the death of your enemies. Instead, you've asked for understanding so that you can do what is right. So I'm going to do what you have asked. I'm giving you a wise and understanding heart so that there will never be anyone like you. I'm also giving you what you haven't asked for— riches and honor—so that no other king will be like

you as long as you live. And if you follow me and obey my laws and commands as your father David did, then I will also give you a long life."[115]

And, that is exactly what happened. Solomon's wisdom was so great that he became known and revered throughout the ancient world. Kings and queens traveled to see him to gain wisdom. And the people of Israel prospered as never before, and never since. Solomon was the greatest ruler in the history of Israel, and perhaps in the entire world. What America needs today is not intelligence, or education, or experience, it is wisdom. And, wisdom is a gift that only God can give.

Consider also the rule of Queen Victoria of Great Britain. Ascending the English throne at age eighteen, Victoria went on to become the greatest monarch in the history of England. And, what was the source of Queen Victoria's wisdom?   That wisdom is perhaps best personified in a portrait that hangs in the National Portrait Gallery in London titled *"The Secret of England's Greatness."*[116]   Set in Windsor Castle, the focus of the painting is Queen Victoria who is presenting a Bible to an unidentified African leader dressed in tribal garb. Some have speculated that the unidentified man in the painting is a former Muslim from Zanzibar. Whether the painting reflects an actual event or is just symbolic of the Queen's deep faith in God is really unimportant. The clear message is that Queen Victoria believed the Bible was the strength and source of the greatness of Great Britain.

Like King Solomon and Queen Victoria, Ben Carson seeks Godly wisdom each day of his life from the Bible. He has read all of it, but he has found particular strength from his daily reading of the book of Proverbs.[117]

In many ways, Dr. Ben Carson is one of the most qualified men to aspire to be president. As noted, very few politicians have faced life and death crises prior to assuming the responsibilities of being president. Even fewer have been personally responsible for making a split second decision that will determine if someone lives or dies. As a pediatric neurosurgeon he has led surgical teams that encountered numerous medical emergencies that called for an instant decision that would either lead to life or to death. Time after time, Dr. Carson made the right decision under extreme pressure. He has a long track record of calmly making the right decision in extremely stressful situations that saved the life of a patient. No profession demands more intelligence and wisdom or causes greater stress than being a neurosurgeon who must often work fast and precisely. Under great pressure, working against the clock, and without any mistakes, the surgeon works to save the life of a patient. In thousands of operations, Dr. Ben Carson has calmly, carefully and wisely reached the right decision that saved a life and restored health. This is the kind of man America needs as our president. Not someone who first worries about the political impact of his decision, but rather a president who is concerned with making a decision that is in the best interest of the American people.

Career politicians in Washington, D.C. and all statewide office holders carry political baggage, even those who have served for just a short period of time in office. They have obligations to special interests that helped them get elected and re-elected. Nearly every senator or congressman from both parties has made use of earmarks to bring home pork to his constituents. They have made deals to help one another get re-elected, but not necessarily to benefit their constituents or the United States of America. They have raised their own salaries, and excluded themselves from laws they voted for and expect us to obey. Politicians have become the ruling class of America. As residents of Washington, D.C. (not their local community) they have isolated themselves from the problems that the average American faces. The United States Congress has even exempted its members and its staff from Obamacare. Politicians no longer see themselves as public servants, but instead, as the masters of the American people.

These *"experienced"* politicians, Democrat and Republican, have brought this nation to the brink of financial collapse through reckless spending that has created a National Debt that will soon reach 20 trillion dollars! They have created bureaucracies that choke the economy with regulations, tell you and me what we should eat, how we should heat our homes, what kind of car we are allowed to drive, even what kind of light bulb we can use. They see themselves as smarter and wiser than we are, and they will continue to add more regulations and pass more laws unless and until a president is elected who says, *"enough, just stop."*

Governors, like senators and congressmen, are deal makers. In fact, even more than members of congress, governors wield great power through patronage. They, too, owe favors to those who helped them get elected.

This is what Ben Carson has to say about high political office being limited to career politicians:

"We've been so brainwashed that we've come to believe that in order to assume a leadership position in this country, you have to have a certain pedigree."

"What's much more important is that you have wisdom...that you have a record of achievement."[118]

Instead of a career politician, America needs a president as envisioned by the Founders, someone who makes a personal sacrifice to serve his fellow citizens. It was the Founders' hope that high public offices would be filled by *"citizen statesmen"* who would use their talents, experience, values and intelligence to bring good government to the American people. They wanted men who didn't see the United States Constitution as an impediment to their gaining power, but rather as a rock solid protection of the rights and freedoms of citizens.

Dr. Ben Carson often speaks of and writes about Dr. Benjamin Rush, one of the five doctors who signed the Declaration of Independence. Dr. Rush was a leading light of the American Revolution. In fact, when Dr. Rush died, he was considered by his contemporaries as being second only to George Washington and Benjamin Franklin among the Founders of our nation. This is what Dr. Rush advised his fellow citizens about public service...

> *"He must love private life, but he must decline no station [office], however public or responsible it may be, when called to it by the suffrages [votes] of his fellow citizens."*[119]

In other words, public office should not be something to be grasped for personal gain and the accrual of power or wealth, but rather something to be called to by your fellow citizens who see in you the character and wisdom to govern wisely. Public office holders were to be public servants, not rulers who intruded into the lives of average Americans.

This is not only the view of Dr. Rush, but virtually of all the Founders. The Founders weren't just lawyers. They were men like George Washington, a successful farmer and military man who was steeped in integrity and virtue. Among their number were ship builders, doctors, merchants, farmers, ministers, inventors, a music composer and men from virtually all walks of life.[120] They were elected president and to congress by their fellow citizens because they were intelligent men of character who could be trusted to abide by the letter and the spirit of the United States Constitution.

Today, congress and the White House are filled with professional politicians—mostly lawyers. Many of these men and women, including President Obama, have never had a private sector job in their life. In other words, they have never worked in a job that provided services or goods in the free market. They have never started a business, met a payroll, managed a project, trained a new hire, lived within a budget or reached a goal to keep their job. Most politicians' understanding of how free enterprise works and how society functions is sorely lacking. Their career is politics, their life is politics, their goal is reelection, and that's why they have created the mess that our nation is now in.

But, some say that the election of citizen statesmen worked out fine in the 1700s when the United States was a small, isolated nation, but it won't work today because the United States is now a world power. They say that we now live in a different world, and the United States is a different nation, with more than 317 million citizens. But, the problems of the world are the problems of men and their relationship to other men. They are the same problems of greed, envy, a lust for power and personal acclamation that have been with the world since the beginning of time. To claim that our challenges today are greater or more complex than those faced by the Founders of our nation or by Abraham Lincoln during the Civil War is simply hubris and ignorance. To say that diminishes the incredible obstacles that the Founders overcame to create this nation and to make it a success. It mocks the resolute courage of

Abraham Lincoln, who refused to let slavery continue and let our nation be torn apart. The Founders and Lincoln faced greater challenges, overcame greater hurdles, and took greater risk than we will probably ever face. The Founders created the United States of America against all odds. Thirteen fledgling colonies defeated the most powerful nation on the face of the earth and then quickly became a world power. Lincoln refused overtures to make peace with the South at the price of continued slavery and a divided nation even when the pressure was intense within his own cabinet for him to do so.

Europeans were astounded that just fifty years after its founding, the United States was competing with the older European nations on every front. Never before in the history of the world had a new nation matured so fast and surpassed nations that had existed for hundreds of years before them. It was virtue and freedom that powered and energized the United States of America and set it apart as an exceptional nation within a very short time span. The United States left the European nations in its dust, as a free and good people reached for the stars.

Human nature has not changed since 1776. Men are still fallible human beings, susceptible to all forms of deceit and debasement. Government is still a dangerous power that must be controlled and limited, lest the freedom of its citizens vanish into a bureaucratic and political nightmare.

The United States of America doesn't need another *"experienced"* career politician as its president. America needs a leader, a person of character who is dedicated to the United States Constitution, and who relies on Godly wisdom. Our president needs to have an understanding of the United States Constitution, an appreciation for the genius and exceptional talents of the American people, a steadfast love of

America, and a philosophy of limited government that guides his decisions and the direction of his presidency. Great presidents have been visionaries and men of good character who led our nation through turbulence and disaster toward that *"shining city on a hill,"* as envisioned by John Winthrop, and often quoted by Ronald Reagan.[121]

Ben Carson has all the makings of a great president. He is humble, he relies on God, and he has been blessed with incredible stamina, intelligence, wisdom and leadership skills. As the head of pediatric neurosurgery at Johns Hopkins University Hospital, he headed up a very large staff that included some of the finest physicians in the world. Some, like Dr. Carson, were humble, but others had huge egos and challenging temperaments that were managed and directed by the calm and wise Dr. Carson. And, under Ben Carson's leadership, cutting edge innovations took place that saved lives and altered the course of medicine throughout the world. And, all the while he was doing this, Dr. Carson continued to operate, continued to write and continued to teach.

No other candidate for the Republican nomination for president has the breadth and depth of executive experience of Ben Carson. Dr. Carson's qualifications to be president are certainly much more extensive and greater than a United States senator, most of whom have very limited executive experience. Make no mistake, a number of United States senators have made very good presidents, just as have a number of men who never served in an elected position prior to being elected president.

And, as far as governors are concerned, only eighteen United States presidents served as a state governor before being elected president. If you limit qualification for president to someone who has served as a governor, you would eliminate John Adams, James Madison, Andrew Jackson, Harry Truman, John Kennedy, and Abraham Lincoln from the list of U.S. presidents. And, let's not forget that Jimmy Carter served two terms as the Governor of Georgia, the ninth most populated state in the nation. Yet, it's almost universally agreed that Jimmy Carter was the most incompetent, unqualified and inept president in the history of the United States. Serving in the United States Senate or serving as governor of a state does not necessarily make an individual more qualified to serve as President of the United States, nor does it make success more likely. The key attributes of a successful president, as General Meese said, are firm principles upon which to base decisions, a clear vision of where you want to lead, an understanding of people, and the power of persuasion that enables a president to bring people together and cause them to follow him. Clearly, the argument that Dr. Benjamin Carson, a visionary surgeon, author and business leader, does not have the necessary qualifications to be president is based on political bias, not reality.

If Abraham Lincoln, a country lawyer who served one term in the United States House of Representatives before becoming president, could hold the nation together during one of the darkest times of our republic, then certainly a dedicated patriot, commonsense Christian, skilled businessman and brilliant brain surgeon has what it takes to serve as United States president during these perilous times. It is the height of arrogance to contend that only an experienced politician has what it takes to serve as president of the United States.

It's like the old joke about the young man who inherited a huge sum of money. This young man wasn't smart, but he was wise enough to know it. So, he decided to use his inheritance to pay for a brain transplant. He went to the brain transplant center and asked what brains were available. The person he spoke with said that they had some incredible brains including an astronaut's brain. The young man asked how much the astronaut's brain cost and he was told nine hundred thousand dollars. Then the brain center spokesman told him about a surgeon's brains that cost a million dollars. Finally, the spokesman told him about politician's brains and said they cost two million dollars. The young man exclaimed that he didn't know politicians were that smart. The spokesman assured him that wasn't the case; it was just that it took so many to have a complete brain.

It's the kind of joke that Ronald Reagan might have told. And, everyone would have understood exactly what he meant. Few would challenge the fact that Ronald Reagan was among the greatest of American presidents.

Great presidents are, most important of all, leaders. They understand that it is not government that is great, but it is the American people, their faith and the freedom they exercise that makes America great. Great presidents, like Ronald Reagan, are guided by simple principles of right and wrong. Their judgment is sound. Like a great doctor, they analyze, they evaluate risk, and then they act, knowing that the fate of the nation lies in their hands. What better person to do such analysis, evaluate risk, and then act than a brilliant, groundbreaking neurosurgeon who carries no political baggage, understands the role of government and appreciates the wisdom of the American people?

Based on his accomplishments, his life experience, his leadership, his political philosophy and his wisdom, it is logical to conclude that Dr. Benjamin Carson will make a great president. The question then becomes what will a Ben Carson presidency look like?

.

Chapter 7
A Ben Carson Presidency

It is, of course, impossible to know precisely what any president will do in office because no one knows what challenges, domestic or international, he or she will face. We already know that Dr. Carson is someone who is calm and steady in a crisis situation. We also know the he understands how to make a life and death decision under extreme pressure. And, we know that he understands how to evaluate risk taking so that the right decision is reached. Ben Carson is not someone that Russian ruler Vladimir Putin could take advantage of. He is not someone that congressional bullies or the news media could push around. He is not someone who would be indecisive in the face of an international crisis.

So, what might we expect during the first 30 days of a Ben Carson administration? Based on his past statements and writings, it's likely that he would first address our dangerous economic position by taking the following actions...

- **10% Across the Board Cuts in Spending.** President Carson will ask members of his cabinet to look deeply into their budgets and offer 10% cuts in spending, eliminating expenditures on nonessential items, i.e. items that do not significantly affect the lives of American citizens.[122] As someone who has risen from poverty, he understands that there is always fat to cut out of even the leanest budget.

- **Health Care Reform.** As a physician, no one knows better than Dr. Carson the importance of the doctor-patient relationship. For more than a year, Dr. Carson has been working with Republican members of Congress to not only repeal Obamacare, but to replace it with a Health Savings Account program that puts the patient in charge of his health care and not some distant bureaucrat.[123] Although it is unlikely this change can be made in the first thirty days, Dr. Carson is prepared, as no other candidate is, to expedite the process of passing a bill that lowers medical costs through tort reform and other commonsense actions.

- **End Taxes on Foreign Earnings.** Ask Congress to pass legislation that would end the double taxation on foreign corporate earnings. This would cause American corporations to bring as much as three trillion dollars back into the U.S. economy. This would instantly spur industry expansion and job growth and make U.S. companies more competitive with foreign firms. Instead of expanding their business in foreign nations, they will then be able to spend that money expanding their business here in the United States.

- **Open Up Land to Oil & Gas Exploration.** Instead of closing off access to U.S. owned land for the exploration of oil and gas, President Carson will reverse this Obama policy, thus creating more jobs, less dependency on foreign oil, and lowering the price of gasoline and heating fuel.

- **Approve the Keystone Pipeline.** With a stroke of the pen, President Carson will create more jobs, cheaper fuel costs, and less dependency on oil from the Middle East by approving the construction of the Keystone Pipeline. But, he will do more than that, Ben Carson will make America truly energy independent.[124]

♦ **Ebola Threat.** As a doctor, no one knows better than Ben Carson how to isolate a disease from the American population. He opposes bringing Ebola patients to the United States.[125] He will encourage the development of a cure for this dreaded disease that will benefit the entire world.

The first 100 days will set the tone for the entire Carson administration. During this period of time Americans can expect commonsense actions such as...

♦ **Terrorism.** Expect a Carson Doctrine to emerge that recognizes that the United States of America is under attack by Islamic extremists around the globe. The purpose of the Carson Doctrine would be to guide the United States to victory in this war without fighting on the enemies' terms.[126] President Carson would not only change the rules of engagement, but would also replace political correctness with common sense by taking the necessary steps to minimize the risk to troops in the field, American citizens, and to our nation.[127]

♦ **Health Savings Accounts.** Repeal the Affordable Care Act and pass a free market Health Savings Account program. This is sure to be high on the Carson agenda. Expect President Carson to receive bi-partisan support for this effort.[128]

♦ **Corporate Tax Rates.** Passage of legislation that lowers corporate income taxes and eliminates tax loopholes and subsidies. Today the United States has the highest corporate tax rates in the world. This burdens American companies, kills American jobs, and makes it more difficult to compete around the globe.

- **Tax Cuts & Tax Reform.** High taxes hurt everyone. Excessively high tax rates like we have today not only hurt workers, they reduce government revenues. When Ronald Reagan passed his historic tax cuts during the first year of his presidency, all Americans benefitted and federal tax revenues soared. That enabled the Republicans in Congress to balance the federal budget. The flatter the tax rates, the fairer they are to all citizens. Carson favors a flat tax that everyone pays. That means that everyone will have skin in the game.[129]

- **Welfare.** Instead of welfare policies that destroy the families of the poor, President Carson is sure to implement programs that provide financial incentives for the poor to keep their families intact and to seek employment, rather than welfare. Working through churches and other nonprofits, President Carson will undoubtedly use the personal knowledge he has of escaping poverty to help those who want to work to find jobs. And, he has expressed his intent to end welfare for those who can work, but choose not to. His policies will embrace the tough love his mother showed to him as he grew up.

- **Cyber Security.** Ben Carson will speed up and streamline American efforts to stop and repel cyber-attacks without encroaching on the freedom or privacy of individuals.

- **NSA Snooping.** President Carson will put an end to eavesdropping on law abiding American citizens without crippling our ability to collect intelligence needed to repel our enemies.

What about judicial appointments and moral leadership? The Founders understood that the republic they created can survive only if elected officials obey the rule of law. When they fail to do so, they encourage all American citizens to ignore the law. This inevitably leads to corruption in government and in society.

One thing is sure to stand out in a Carson presidency and that is American unity.[130] There will be no efforts to set Americans against each other in the Carson administration. Instead you can expect Ben Carson to use his powers of persuasion to bring Americans together. Ben Carson will lead the nation toward a truly post racial society, where men and women are judged by the content of their character, not by the color of their skin, thus fulfilling the dream of Dr. Martin Luther King, Jr. Political opponents will be treated as opponents, not enemies. Political speeches, debates and discussions will be honest, civil and respectful. Moral values and the principles of the Founders will be respected and encouraged.

More than any president since Ronald Reagan, Ben Carson reveres and respects the wisdom of the Founders and the United States Constitution. For judicial appointments he will seek out men and women who are equally dedicated to the spirit, as well as the letter, of our Constitution.

Furthermore, President Ben Carson will, during his time in office, shrink the size of government, giving people more power over their lives, and less power to government bureaucrats. He will not only balance the budget, but also begin paying down the National Debt so that the United States is not subject to blackmail by rogue nations like China or Russia. He has expressed a long term desire to tie the value of the dollar to gold, thus making it more difficult for politicians to revert to their past practices of spending money we do not have. And, in regard to spending, Ben Carson is sure to support a balanced budget amendment to the United States Constitution so that never again can politicians put the future of our children and grandchildren in jeopardy.

Ben Carson is a man of character. He's not a radical who believes in manipulating the American people, nor does he want to remake America into a socialist nation. He believes in America and he believes in the American people. He knows and understands that American citizens have more good sense and wisdom about how to live their own lives than do Washington, D.C. bureaucrats.

Honesty and integrity will be the hallmarks of the Carson administration.   Ben Carson will not tolerate scandals like those that have originated in the Obama administration. He will not lie or dissemble. He will not blame others for his own mistakes.   In that regard especially, he will be a president like America's first president, George Washington.

Finally, by the way he lives his own life, the wisdom he speaks, and the strength of character he brings to the Oval Office, President Ben Carson will set a new moral tone for our nation based on traditional values. Ben Carson will be a man we will be proud to call Mr. President.

Chapter 8
Carson vs. Clinton

Although Hillary Clinton is the frontrunner for the Democrat presidential nomination, that does not guarantee that she will indeed be the 2016 standard bearer of the Democrat Party. Senator Elizabeth Warren, former Senator James Webb, former Maryland Governor Martin O'Malley, and Vice President Joe Biden are all considering a run for the White House. As you may recall, Hillary was the frontrunner for the Democrat nomination in 2008, but she lost that race. Democrat voters may be looking for a new face, a new leader; but nevertheless the odds-on-favorite to win the Democrat nomination in 2016 is former Secretary of State Hillary Clinton.

So, for the purpose of speculation, let's suppose that Hillary Clinton wins the 2016 Democrat Party nod for a run for the White House. If that happens, how will Ben Carson stack up against Hillary? And, if Hillary Clinton wins the White House, will her administration look more like that of Bill Clinton or more like that of Barack Obama?

Let's look at a Hillary Clinton White House first. On the surface of the matter, lots of folks will anticipate that her administration would look much like that of Bill's; on the left of the political spectrum, but not as extreme as Obama, willing to compromise with the Republicans, not as ideological as the Obama administration, and perhaps stronger on defense.

Unfortunately, that is not what we should expect from a Hillary Clinton administration. Hillary Clinton is no Bill Clinton. Hillary, like Obama, is a disciple of the far left, more than slightly thuggish, Saul Alinsky. In fact, Hillary wrote her 92 page honors thesis at Wellesley on Alinsky.[131] After Bill Clinton was elected president, someone from the White House called one of Hillary's professors and asked Wellesley to make her paper unavailable to the public. They complied with this request. However, in recent years, a copy of her paper has made its way into the public. This is what she said in the conclusion of her paper about Saul Alinsky...

> *"If the ideals Alinsky espouses were actualized, the result would be social revolution... Alinsky is regarded by many as the proponent of a dangerous socio/political philosophy. As such he has been feared—just as Eugene Debs or Walt Whitman or Martin Luther King has been feared, because each embraced the most radical of political faiths—democracy."*[132]

Hillary not only read Alinsky, she met him on three occasions and was, in fact, offered a job by him in her senior year. This is the dedication to Lucifer that Alinsky wrote in his book...

> *"...the very first radical [who] rebelled against the establishment and did it so effectively, that he at least won his own kingdom."*[133]

Both Obama and Clinton are acolytes of Alinsky, although they believe in a radical transformation of America from within, rather than from without as proposed by their mentor. Like Alinsky, both justify being mendacious because they both believe that the ends justify the means. Hillary Clinton is simply not Bill Clinton. A Hillary Clinton administration will not be a continuation of the presidency of Bill Clinton; it will be a continuation of the radical Obama administration. As author Dinesh D'Souza puts it...

> *"If Hillary Clinton is elected in 2016, the baton will have passed from one Alinskyite to another. In this*

case, Alinsky's influence will have taken on a massive, almost unimaginable, importance. Obama will have had eight years to remake America, and Hillary will have another four or perhaps eight to complete the job. Together, these two have the opportunity to largely undo the nation's founding ideals. They will have had the power, and the time, to unmake and then remake America. They may not be responsible for the suicide of America, but they certainly will have helped to finish off a certain way of life in America, and they will leave us with a country unrecognizable not only to Washington and Jefferson but also to those of us who grew up in the twentieth century. If they succeed there may be no going back. Then it will be their America, not ours, and we will be a people bereft of a country, with no place to go."[134]

The truth is, whether you call yourself a liberal, or you identify yourself as an Alinsky radical, you hold in common the same philosophy of government, power. The pro America liberals of the 1960s like John F. Kennedy, Henry "Scoop" Jackson, Estes Kefauver, and Harry Truman, are gone from the Democrat Party. They have been replaced with radicals like Obama, Clinton and Warren, who reject the principles of the Founders, and instead seek to tear down our society and completely remake it. The roots of the modern Democrat Party lie not with Thomas Jefferson, as they like to claim, but rather with Jean-Jacques Rousseau, whose ideas inspired the French Revolution. Rousseau hated religion and, like today's radicals, sought to create a society free of religion and of traditional moral values. Rousseau honestly believed that true freedom could only exist in a society free of the influence of faith in God. However, when French society became untethered from faith and traditional moral values, it quickly degenerated into a bloody, brutal and cruel dictatorship.

Individual freedom vanished, and the citizens of France lived in fear during the reign of terror that a society free of God always results in.

Today's radicals who have captured the Democrat Party do not desire such a nation, but neither do they fear it. After all, Obama's mentors include the one time Communist Party member, Frank Marshall Davis. Obama was introduced to Davis by his maternal grandfather, Stanley Dunham, who asked Davis to mentor the young Obama. Davis was not only a card carrying Communist (#47544) who had sworn allegiance to the Soviet Union, many consider him to be the ideological father of Barack Obama.[135] Obama's mentors also include his close friend, Bill Ayers, the terrorist who bombed the Pentagon and the United States Capitol building. Ayers, who assisted Obama down the political path, has an ideological lineage that goes straight back to Lenin, Hitler, Pol Pot and Robespierre, who led the French Reign of Terror. Obama, Clinton, Warren, Ayers, et al. do not understand that individual freedom can only exist when government and government power is limited and discrete. Neither do they understand that individual liberty can only reign supreme when law stands above the whims of man, and man stands in awe of God.

Ben Carson asked a very important question...
"Why are they [secular progressives] so determined to remove God from our lives?"[136]
And, then he answered his own question...
"They recognize that if we have no higher authority to answer to than man, we become gods unto ourselves and get to determine our own behavior. In their world, 'If it feels good, do it.' They can justify anything based on their ideology because in their opinion, there is no higher authority other than themselves to overrule them. They have a visceral

reaction to the mention of God's word, because it tears at the fabric of their justification system."[137]

Historian Paul Kengor eloquently explained the linkage between faith and freedom...

"...to invoke freedom alone is a mistake. Freedom by itself, isolated, is libertarianism, not conservatism. For the conservative, freedom requires faith; it should never be decoupled from faith. Freedom not rooted in faith can lead to moral anarchy, which, in turn, creates social and cultural chaos. Freedom without faith is the Las Vegas Strip, not the City of God. Freedom without faith begets license and invites vice rather than virtue. Faith infuses the soul with a sanctifying grace that allows humans in a free society to love and serve their neighbors, to think about more than themselves. We aspire to our better angels when our faith nurtures and elevates our free will."[138]

Of course, the Founders understood this when they wrote and spoke about the importance of virtue to the continuous existence of a free society. Benjamin Franklin wrote cogently...

"...only a virtuous people are capable of freedom. As nations become corrupt and vicious, they have more need of masters."[139]

Another Founder, John Adams, wrote repeatedly about the importance of virtue to sustaining a free republic...

"Statesmen... may plan and speculate for liberty, but it is religion and morality alone, which can establish the principles upon which freedom can securely stand. The only foundation of a free constitution is pure virtue, and if this cannot be inspired into our people, in a greater measure, than they have it now, they may change their rulers and the forms of government, but they will

not obtain a lasting liberty. They will only exchange tyrants or tyrannies."[140]

Other Founders, including George Washington and Patrick Henry, made similar comments about the importance of religion, virtue, and morality. These men understood the failings of human nature that was common to all men and women. It is the misunderstanding of human nature that lies at the root of all the mischief caused by liberalism and its progeny, left wing radicalism. As the late Charles Colson explained it...

> *"The denial of our sinful nature, and the utopian myth it breeds, leads not to beneficial social experiments but to tyranny. The confidence that humans are perfectible provides a justification for trying to make them perfect...no matter what it takes. And with God out of the picture, those in power are not accountable to any higher authority. They can use any means necessary, no matter how brutal or coercive, to remold people to fit their notion of the perfect society.*"[141]

Colson and the Founders understood that all men and women live in a fallen state. They knew that imperfect people could not exercise self-restraint that comes only from fear and awe of God. They also understood that compassion would die if the new nation ceased to be populated by a virtuous people who were led by God to care for their fellow man. And, of course, the Founders understood that a free society cannot be sustained without self-restraint. A society free of moral restraint and unmotivated by a love for their fellow citizens is incapable of governing itself and sustaining a free society.

Today President Obama complains about the fact that the Founders created a Constitution of divided and limited powers. During a radio interview in 2001 he complained...

"But the Supreme Court never ventured into the issues of redistribution of wealth and sort of more basic issues of political and economic justice in this society. And to that extent as radical as people tried to characterize the Warren court, it wasn't that radical. It didn't break free from the essential constraints that were placed by the founding fathers in the Constitution, at least as it's been interpreted, and the Warren court interpreted it in the same way that generally the Constitution is a charter of negative liberties. It says what the states can't do to you, it says what the federal government can't do to you, but it doesn't say what the federal government or the state government must do on your behalf."[142]

As president he has repeatedly tried to ignore the rule of law by bypassing Congress and ignoring the Constitution. Every time he succeeds, he erodes the foundation of our free society. The course that today's Democrat Party is on is a dangerous one. It leads down a slippery slope that can only result in bigger government and less freedom. All of America's Founders worried that future generations would fritter away the freedom that they had won with their treasure, their honor and their blood. They understood that a nation's grasp on freedom is a tenuous one. John Adams put it this way...

"A Constitution of Government once changed from Freedom, can never be restored. Liberty, once lost, is lost forever."[143]

This is what Ben Carson is talking about when he speaks of the decline of our nation. We have forgotten the foundation of freedom. We are abandoning the idea of a limited government, where the people are supreme. In contrast, Ben Carson firmly believes in the principles of the Founders. Sadly, that is no longer true of the Democrat Party in the 21st Century.

Unlike the Republican Party that enunciates a philosophy of limited government that appeals to and benefits all Americans, the Democrat Party is, by design, a party of coalitions. Using a model first utilized by Franklin D. Roosevelt, the Democrats have cunningly cobbled together a political party that is made up of groups that often have opposing interests. As a party, the Democrats appeal to the basest instincts of the individual—jealously, envy, anger and greed. Their operating political philosophy is to divide and conquer.

As the leaders of today's Democrat Party see it, individuals are only important as part of a voting bloc that can benefit their political objectives. So, instead of thinking of Americans as diverse individuals created by God who are each unique in their own right, the Democrats only think of them as a member of some aggrieved group. Accordingly, they see each group as a collection of victims that need the aid and assistance of the Democrat Party. In other words, the members of the Democrat coalition aren't special and unique in their own right, they are only important as a member of a group that will help the radicals who control the Democrat Party gain power.

At its core, the modus operandi of today's Democrat Party is nothing more or less than cynical class warfare. As long as the Democrat Party continues to set one group of people against another, there will never be unity in the United States. The reality is that today's Democrat Party leaders have no genuine compassion or caring for the individuals within the groups in their coalition; they see them only as pawns to be manipulated to advance the overarching goal of gaining total political power in the United States.

Their approach is Marxist, an ideology whose lineage is inspirationally linked to the French Revolution. From the

beginning, Lenin saw people as only members of groups—
the bourgeois, the proletariat, etc. Within the proletariat
were the farmers, the workers and others who had
legitimate grievances who were exploited by Lenin, Trotsky
and others to gain power. Like today's Democrats, there
was no genuine compassion or caring about individuals
within these groups; they were simply a means to the
acquisition of power.

And, once Lenin gained power, the economic and
personal status of individuals within these groups did not
improve; it became permanently shackled to the unending
misery of the Communist slave state. Similarly, the
Democrats have created a permanent welfare underclass
that has been restrained through laws, regulations, poor
education, and other governmental measures from
advancing up the economic ladder. In truth, the Democrats
gain no political advantage by helping those on welfare to
escape poverty and become economically self-sufficient.
Once free of poverty and welfare, the ability of the
Democrats to manipulate these individuals as a group
would be greatly diminished.

And, as long as the Democrats remain in power, there
will be no path to economic freedom and success for those
trapped in poverty. In fact, as government becomes more
powerful and pervasive, the ranks of the poor will swell,
prosperity will decline, and freedom will shrink for all.

In stark contrast to the Democrats' message of bigger
and more powerful government and less individual
freedom, Ben Carson's message is that of the Founders—
more individual freedom, more personal responsibility,
and more opportunity. Carson's pro-freedom message is
one that benefits every individual in society. Carson's
commitment to individual freedom is not just

philosophical; it is a bone deep outgrowth of his personal experience. It is a deep understanding of the blessing of freedom that only those who have escaped government-fostered poverty can truly appreciate.

Ben Carson's message is a true, clear and experience based message of hope and opportunity. It is not the false siren song of the left that leads to less freedom, less opportunity and eventually to chains and slavery.

The implementation of the Carson agenda means more jobs, easier access to the ladder of success and the accessibility of the American Dream by all Americans who are willing to learn and work hard.

It means a return to the Founders' belief in a virtuous society, one that relies on faith in God, as the Founders enumerated in the Declaration of Independence, and as proclaimed on our currency. It means leadership in the White House that is not guided by cynical political considerations, but by what actions are in the best interest of the United States of America.

It means leadership that strives for American unity, not division. It means a society that seeks assimilation of all Americans, instead of the Balkanization of America.[144] It means leadership that encourages personal compassion and honor.

It means pride in America's achievements, the rule of law, the United States Constitution and respecting the values and insight of America's Founders. It means a renewed belief in American exceptionalism, and John Winthrop's vision of America as a *"shining city on a hill."*[145]

It means discarding *"political correctness"* that keeps Americans from solving problems, and that violates the foundational principles of free speech. It means the end of dissembling and lies to the American people by America's political leaders. And it means a president who takes responsibility for errors made, and doesn't always try to blame someone else.

It means a return to civility in public discourse and between those who hold opposite positions on public policy.

It means the restoration of respect for America around the globe and the end of bowing and scraping to petty dictators. It means no more apologies for the achievements and greatness of America.

It means a restoration of commonsense economic policies, including a balanced budget and a dramatic reduction in our National Debt. It means lower tax rates and a tax system in which everyone participates.

It means an administration that lives within the rule of law and respects the importance of the separation of powers. It means a government that protects the rights of all citizens, including the unborn.

It means a government that fulfills its enumerated role of defending and protecting the United States of America from enemies foreign and domestic. It means peace through strength.

It means an end to politically motivated scandals that seek to use the power of government to punish the opponents of those elected to serve. It means fidelity to American ambassadors and other U.S. representatives around the globe.

It means faithfulness to those in the United States military who put their lives on the line to protect and defend our nation.

It means a nonpolitical Department of Justice that seeks equal justice for all and that sets the standard for operating within the law.

It means the appointment of federal judges that are dedicated to the spirit and the letter of the United States Constitution, not to rewriting it to mean something other than what the originators of the Constitution intended.

It means an American dollar that is sound, strong and backed by gold.

It means a president who sets the standard for morality and good behavior. It means honesty and integrity in government and real transparency of actions by the president. It means a renewed emphasis on character and traditional values.

It means being an ally that keeps its word and can be trusted to do the right thing, even when the right thing is the difficult thing. It means the use of military power only when that is the last resort. And, if it becomes necessary to use military force, it means a non-proportional response to any attacks on the United States of America or its allies.[146] It means understanding that appeasement only leads to a larger war, a greater loss of life and to the success of America's enemies.

And, finally, it means a president who loves America deeply, and respects her traditions, her philosophical foundations, and her history.

If that's the kind of nation you believe in, then Ben Carson is the right choice for you in 2016.

Today, many months before the November 2016 presidential election, most polls and surveys show Ben Carson as one of the strongest prospective candidates against Hillary Clinton. These polls are so early that not too much stock can be placed in their accuracy, but they are an indication of the broad and deep support that Ben Carson has from all Americans—black, white, Hispanic, Asian—who see in him the opportunity to elect a talented, well-educated and experienced man who will govern wisely in the shadow of the Founders and with great respect for American traditions and for the United States Constitution.

Chapter 9
Ben Carson on the Issues

Where does Dr. Benjamin Carson stand on the critical issues of the day? In his own words, this is where he stands on the following issues:

Abortion

Ben Carson's tenacious commitment to life is evident in this recounting of an exchange with the head of the American Civil Liberties Union (ACLU) on the issue of abortion...

> *"I asked him if he would speak for and defend the rights of a twenty-eight-week-old baby (born prematurely) who was in an incubator and on life support. He replied that that was a no-brainer; of course the ACLU would defend such an individual... I then asked why it was difficult to defend a baby that was five weeks further along in development and was in the most protected environment possible, but easy to defend a less viable individual who was outside the womb."—* America the Beautiful, pages 99 & 100

> *"How can a society that kills millions of innocent unborn babies and then labels anyone opposing the practice as 'anti-woman' claim even a modicum of goodness? How can a nation that uses its news media to subtly trash traditional families, promote a drug-filled lifestyle, and ridicule faith in God claim the mantle of righteousness?"—The Washington Times,* April 16, 2014

> *"According to God's word, life begins at conception rather than at the time of delivery or at some arbitrary point during gestation."*

"In the Book of Exodus, chapter 21, verses 22-24, it is made quite clear that God considers the life of the unborn to be just as valuable as the life of an adult. When you couple this belief with the commandment, 'Thou shalt not kill' (Exodus 20:13), it is clear that abortion is rarely a moral option."—One Nation, page 193

American Compassion

"When disasters occur in other countries, who is first on the scene with massive aid? The United States, of course. It does not matter whether the mishap befalls a friend or an enemy, we are always there. It doesn't matter whether it's a very poor country like Haiti or a very rich country such as Japan, we are still always there. Our compassion for and aid to other countries is unprecedented in the history of the world."—America the Beautiful, pages 183-184

American Exceptionalism

"...there has never been another nation like the United States of America. Yes, we have made mistakes, but we continue to learn from them, and as long as we remain capable of embracing life, liberty, and the pursuit of happiness as our goal, and we are willing to guarantee those things to our citizens, I believe we will continue to grow in greatness."—America the Beautiful, page 194

American Generosity

"America has been and continues to be the most generous nation on earth. We love to help the less fortunate, and I hope we always care for our fellow man."—The Washington Times, July 17, 2013

American Greatness

"Although it was an arduous road filled with obstacles and grueling hours, I was able to realize

my dream because of the generous freedoms we enjoy here in our nation. It is this ability of anyone to achieve their dreams that is perhaps the greatest thing about America."—America the Beautiful, page 184

American Leadership

"It is time to set aside political correctness and replace it with the bold values and principles that founded our nation and caused it to race to the pinnacle of the world faster than any other nation in history. It is time to stop apologizing and to start leading, because the world is desperately in need of fair and ethical leadership. If that leader is not America, who will it be, and where will they lead?"—America the Beautiful, page 195

American Unity

"The word 'racism' is tossed around so easily by those intent on creating division and victimhood instead of unity."—The Washington Times, July 24, 2013

Balancing the Budget

"I believe the logical approach would be to have each governmental agency and department trim its budget by 10 percent—with no exceptions. In each subsequent year, another 10 percent decrease would be required and would continue as long as necessary to bring the budget back into balance."— America the Beautiful, page 109

Border Security

"I do think that it is necessary to secure the border. We need to have control over who is in our country, we need to know who they are, and what they're doing here."—Newsmax, June 2014

Capitalism

"The concept of rewards for production lies at the foundation of capitalism and needs to be understood. The anticipation of rewards for being productive and the fear of consequences for being unproductive are great human motivators for both young and old. Historically, when these motivators are removed, productivity declines. Nonproductive people frequently make excuses for their lack of production, and as long as they can utilize those excuses, they have no reason to change their ways. But motivate them and watch what happens."—
America the Beautiful, pages 74 and 75

Civil Rights and Racism

"Although much overt racism has been eliminated in America, there are still too many people who make sweeping generalizations about whole groups of people based on a negative encounter with a person of a different race. In order to resolve this problem, we must first admit that it exists even in our own families or ourselves—and African-Americans are just as likely to harbor racist attitudes as white people."—America the Beautiful, page 117

"I found that it was Republicans who were responsible for the abolition of slavery and for the passage of the Civil Rights Act. I also began to realize that it was not political biases that were largely responsible for the plight of African-Americans in our nation, but rather racist attitudes. After the many gains realized through the civil rights movement, racist people from both parties adopted a paternalistic attitude toward African-Americans and enacted federal and state programs designed to take care of people who couldn't take care of themselves—people who were

ignorant, stupid, or just plain lazy. In the process of being 'do-gooders,' both Republicans and Democrats removed much of the drive and determination from innumerable African-Americans, who found it easier to accept government charity than continue on a path of hard work and self-reliance."—America the Beautiful, page 157

Class Warfare

"Class warfare is an artificial division created for political advantage, and it should be rejected outright by the American people—for we have far too many real problems to devote energy to artificial ones."—America the Beautiful, page 161

National Debt

"To saddle the next generation with unimaginable debt is not only callous, it is morally reprehensible. How can we even live with ourselves knowing that we are eroding the standard of living of the next generations with each dollar that we add to the national debt?"—America the Beautiful, page 108

"It is hard to believe that our leaders in both political parties do not understand that they are jeopardizing the financial future of the next generations by allowing continued debt accumulation, even if they are slowing the rise of the debt."—One Nation, page 73

Ebola

"I [am]...not comfortable with the idea of bringing infected individuals into our midst when we can readily treat them elsewhere. We can happily receive them back once the infectious danger has passed. When one does a logical benefit-to-risk analysis, it is clear that the worst things that could happen by intentionally bringing this dangerous

disease to America are far worse than the best things that could happen."—The Washington Times, October 9, 2014

Education

"When we instill morals and values into the educational process for young people, however, we help them realize they have an obligation to become well educated and informed citizens, and to contribute to the system as opposed to draining it of its resources. Public prayer and discussion of common principles that strengthen society's moral fabric are essential to establishing an atmosphere of courtesy and decency. The renowned Noah Webster said, 'Society requires that the education of youth should be watched with the most scrupulous attention. Education, in a great measure, forms the moral characters of men, and morals are the basis of government."—America the Beautiful, page 59

"Reading was emphasized so strongly among the early settlers of America that anyone finishing the second or third grade was completely literate, as is borne out in the absolutely beautiful prose that characterized the writing style and letters received from the Western frontiers of America in the early 19th century."—The Washington Times, July 16, 2014

Energy Independence

"Several administrations have talked about the importance of energy independence, yet we remain as dependent on foreign oil as we were years ago."
"It is estimated that the amount of oil in the Dakotas and Montana is eight times greater than the amount of oil in Saudi Arabia."—One Nation, page 149

"I thoroughly believe that we have a duty to protect our environment not only for ourselves but for the next generations. However, we also have a duty to develop our economic potential and free ourselves of unnecessary stress and dependency on volatile foreign sources of energy. As a bonus, energy independence for us means decreased revenues for radical terrorist elements who aim to destroy our way of life."—One Nation, page 150

"Expanding our wealth of energy resources, as well as encouraging development of new renewable energy sources can provide an enormous economic lift with obvious benefits, but it can also bolster our role as a formidable player in the struggle for world leadership."—The Washington Times, March 26, 2014

Entitlements

"The only reason I can imagine that it would be a good idea for government to foster dependency in large groups of citizens is to cultivate a dependable voting bloc that will guarantee continued power as long as the entitlements are provided. The problem of course is that such a government will eventually 'run out of other people's money,' as Margaret Thatcher once famously said."—One Nation, page 158

Executive Experience

"Through my budget-management experiences as a division director at Johns Hopkins for many years, and through many tough financial experiences as the president and co-founder of the Carson Scholars Fund, which is active in all 50 states, I gained enormous knowledge of business practices, but that pales in significance to what I have learned as a board member of both Costco and the Kellogg

Company during the past 17 years. Managing and growing large multinational corporations requires wisdom and experience, and I have enjoyed the opportunity to work with and learn from both politically liberal and conservative business executives."—The Washington Times, July 23, 2014

Executive Orders

"This immature behavior is vividly exhibited by President Obama in his shameless use of executive orders to try to force the eventual success of Obamacare. Administration supporters defend his strategy by pointing out that previous presidents have even more executive orders than Mr. Obama. It's like saying that punching someone 40 times is more harmful than shooting him four times."—The Washington Times, February 26, 2014

Faith

"Jesus clearly instructed his followers that a crucial part of their Christian life was living out his teachings in everyday life and sharing the good news of faith with others. Not being willing to talk about my faith would mean disregarding His specific teaching."—Take the Risk, page 132

Fiscal Policy

"The stark reality is that if we don't immediately assume fiscal responsibility and adopt policies that are conducive to economic growth, an economic disaster will ensure that will affect all generations."—One Nation, page 59

"Since Franklin D. Roosevelt decoupled the U.S. dollar from gold, our currency has been backed only by our good name. Not only has this resulted in fiscal policy problems, but it has also steadily increased the gap between the wealth of the rich and the poor in this country and provided the

opportunity to do a lot of fancy currency manipulation. Nothing good will happen if we continue along this reckless course of fiscal irresponsibility."—One Nation, page 75

Fortitude and Freedom

"Every time I see our magnificent Stars and Stripes, I think of the fortitude of those Americans at Fort McHenry who, although outnumbered and outgunned, never allowed that flag to lower in surrender. That should remind us of who we are: a people who never surrender, who never give up, who are historically rooted in a faith in God rather than in the vicissitudes of man, who believe in freedom, and who would rather die than abandon our beliefs in equality and justice for everyone."— America the Beautiful, page 187

Future

"I am thoroughly convinced that Americans with common sense will soon regain power in this nation."—The Washington Times, May 28, 2014

"I am convinced that the dreams of our Founders of a free nation filled with knowledgeable and caring people who trust in God and accept personal responsibility is still possible."—The Washington Times, July 16, 2014

Immigration

"The overwhelming majority of Americans want the southern borders of our country secured and our immigration laws enforced, but several administrations recently have been unwilling to get tough on this issue because they do not want to alienate a large voting block of Latinos. This is yet another area where our government's leadership and the wishes of many of the people diverge and

the people are being ignored."—*America the Beautiful*, page 39

"As long as we reward people who break laws, they will continue to break laws. We do need a continual flow of immigrants, but choosers need not be beggars. We [must] make decisions based on our needs."—The Washington Times, June 18, 2014

"A national guest worker program makes sense and seems to work well in Canada. Non-citizens would have to apply for a guest-worker permit and have a guaranteed job awaiting them. Taxes would be paid at a rate commensurate with other U.S. workers and special visas would allow for easy entry and egress across borders. Guest-worker status would be granted to individuals and not to groups. People already here illegally could apply for guest-worker status from outside of the country. This means they would have to leave first. They should in no way be rewarded for having broken our laws... When they return they still would not be U.S. citizens, but they would be legal, and they would be paying taxes. Only jobs that are vacant as a result of a lack of interest by American citizens should be eligible for the guest-worker program."—The Washington Times, June 18, 2014

Jobs

"If, instead of regulating and taxing to death the engine of growth, our government suddenly decided to leave it alone and allow it to be nourished by free market forces, like the seed, it would explode with vibrant growth, jobs would return quickly, and to the pleasant surprise of the government, its own coffers would fill, because the tax base would be broadened. As an added bonus, the obligations of the government would lessen because there would be

fewer citizens on the dole. This would make it possible to reduce, and eventually eliminate the National Debt. If our government could learn to create a nourishing environment for entrepreneurial endeavors rather than gorging itself on the fruits of their labor, a win-win situation would ensue."—The Washington Times, January 15, 2014

Judeo-Christian Values

"Our Judeo-Christian values led this nation to the pinnacle of the world in record time. If we embrace them, they will keep us there."

"Second Chronicles 7:14 says, 'If my people, which are called by my name, shall humble themselves and pray, and seek my face and turn from their wicked ways, then will I hear from heaven, and will forgive their sins and will heal their land.'"—The Washington Times, February 12, 2014

Junk Science

"DDT was banned for use as an insecticide in 1972 because some experts thought it might pose a carcinogenic risk. There was no clear evidence that it actually caused cancer in humans, though there was some basis for thinking it might. For caution's sake, farmers and others needing to control insect populations were forced to switch to organophosphate insecticides (sure as parathions), some of which were eventually proven to be hundreds, even thousands of times more toxic that the DDT they replaced."—Take the Risk, page 60

Marriage

"...I believe marriage is between a man and a woman and that no group has the right to change the definition of marriage to suit their needs."—One Nation, page 18

"As a Bible-believing Christian, you might imagine that I would not be a proponent of gay marriage. I believe God loves homosexuals as much as he loves everyone, but if we can redefine marriage as between two men or two women or any other way based on social pressures as opposed to between a man and a woman, we will continue to redefine it in any way that we wish, which is a slippery slope with a disastrous ending, as witnessed in the dramatic fall of the Roman Empire."—America the Beautiful, page 182

Obamacare

*"You know Obamacare is really I think the worst thing that has happened in this nation since slavery. And ... it is slavery in a way, because it is making all of us subservient to the government, and it was never about health care. It was about control."—*2013 Value Voters Summit

"The implications of such a shift of power (where we have no choice but to purchase the only prescribed product—Obamacare), are profound in a society that is supposed to be free and centered around freedom of choice. Once we give the government this kind of power, it is naïve to believe that they will stop here in their quest for total control of our lives."—One Nation, pages 12 & 13

"I have stated in the past that Obamacare is the worst thing to occur in our country since slavery. Why did I make such a strong statement? Obviously I recognize the horrors of slavery. My roots have been traced back to Africa, and I am aware of some horrendous deeds inflicted on my ancestors in this country." "The purpose of the statement was not to minimize the most evil institution in American history, but rather to draw

attention to a profound shift of power from the people to the government."

"I think this shift is beginning to wrench the nation from one centered on the rights of individual citizens to one that accepts the right of the government to control even the most essential parts of our lives. This strikes a serious blow to the concept of freedom that gave birth to this nation."

"Some well-known radicals have very publicly written and stated that in order for their idea of utopian, egalitarian society to emerge in the United States, the government must control health care, which ensures the dependency of the populace on government. Historical analysis of many countries that have gone this route demonstrates obliteration of the middle class and massive expansion of the poor, dependent class with a relatively small number of elites in control."—Newsmax, March 19, 2014

"...I believe everyone should have a health savings account (HSA) and an electronic medical record (EMR) at the time of birth as a first step toward reform. The EMR should only be in the patient's possession in the form of an electronic chip embedded into a card or device that can be shared with a health care provider at the patient's discretion. It would not be available to the IRS or any other governmental agency, and the database would of course need to be as secure as possible to protect personal information from hackers. The HSA could be populated with funds supplied by an employer, the owner, relatives, friends, and governmental sources."—One Nation, pages 143-144

"...it would only be necessary for the government to make contributions in the cases of individuals incapable of making a living."—One Nation, page 144

"With each person owning his own HSA in the United States, most people would become interested in saving by shopping for the most cost-effective high-quality health care plans available. This would bring the entire health care industry into the free-market economic model resulting in price transparency and creating a system where services and pricing are more closely related to value."—One Nation, page 144

"Since most of the relationships would be doctor-patient relationships, the doctors certainly would not order things without regard to price, and patients would not permit excessive depletion of their HSA's by careless expenditure. With everybody becoming cost conscious, price transparency would be of paramount importance and fair competition would cause prices to be consistent and reasonable."—One Nation, page 145

"In essence, this would make each family unit its own private health insurance company with no unnecessary middleman increasing costs. It would also make it possible for people to pass the money in their HSAs to family members at the time of their death."—One Nation, page 145

Political Correctness

"It is time to set aside political correctness and replace it with the bold values and principles that founded our nation and caused it to race to the pinnacle of the world faster than any other nation in history. It is time to stop apologizing and to start leading, because the world is desperately in need of fair and ethical leadership. If that leader is not America, then who will it be, and where will they lead?"—America the Beautiful, page 195

"Many people equate political correctness with kind and compassionate speech. The two things are vastly different with very different purposes. Political correctness is meant to control thought patterns and speech content, creating unanimity and societal conformity, while kind and compassionate speech is meant to take into consideration the feelings and circumstances of others without compromising the truth. It is a much better alternative. We need to be wary of those who attempt to convince groups of people that they should be offended by a word, phrase or symbol instead of concentrating on the real message being conveyed.—The Washington Times, June 25, 2014

Poverty and Compassion

"Compassion... should mean providing a mechanism to escape poverty rather than simply maintaining people in an impoverished state by supplying handouts."

"...but I do not believe the government has any obligation to take care of able-bodied citizens who are capable of providing for themselves."

"The only reason I can imagine that it would be a good idea for government to foster dependency in large groups of citizens is to cultivate a dependable voting bloc that will guarantee continued power as long as the entitlements are provided. The problem of course is that such a government will eventually 'run out of other people's money,' as Margaret Thatcher once famously said."—One Nation, pages 157 & 158

"One logical and compassionate solution to the problem of growing welfare rolls is to set a date several years away for the elimination of welfare payments for able bodied individuals who could work and support themselves."

"...continuing to sustain people in a dependent position with meager welfare payments is what is really cruel, because it frequently removes the incentive to engage in self-improvement activities."—One Nation, page 161

Republicans and Democrats

"Each of these parties [Republicans and Democrats] has been engaged in the gradual but consistent growth of the central government and its claim on power. Ever-expanding programs offering benefits to the masses are difficult to resist, and with the proliferation of the new media it also became possible for elected officials to gain great notoriety and power. This power became addicting to many elected officials... who wanted to hold their positions for extended periods of time—even for life."—America the Beautiful, page 24

"Both Democrats and Republicans have strayed so far from the path of responsible financial policy that the concept of balancing the budget is foreign to them. I believe many of them simply cannot grasp the concept of only spending what you have. I do understand that making budgetary cuts will be painful, but it will not be nearly as painful as going bankrupt!"—America the Beautiful, page 108

"Politically, elitism knows no single party. Establishing policies that create dependency, like easy food stamps and subsidized health care for families making in excess of $80,000 per year, seems to stroke the egos of both Republican and Democrat elites who believe they are God's gift to mankind."—One Nation, page 29

"Black leaders like Booker T. Washington, George Washington Carver, and Dr. Martin Luther King,

Jr, among others, were great proponents of self-reliance and self-help."

"Many of the elites from both parties embrace these men as heroes but propose social policies that do not encourage self-reliance; policies these men would never have approved. Based on their policies, I believe that they subconsciously think that some people are not capable of helping themselves."—One Nation, page 30

"It is hard to believe that our leaders in both political parties do not understand that they are jeopardizing the financial future of the next generations by allowing continued debt accumulation, even if they are slowing the rise of that debt."—One Nation, page 73

"The fact that the Republican Party in particular often seems to stand for principle, only to cave in to pressure at the last minute, has turned off a huge number of voters. A true reformation of the Republican Party would be a breath of fresh air for those voters."—One Nation, page 177

Second Amendment

"The Second Amendment was crafted by wise citizens who recognized how quickly an enemy invasion could occur or how our own government could be deceived into thinking it had the right to dominate the people. Such domination is considerably more difficult when people have arms and can put up significant resistance. This is the reason that brutal dictators like Fidel Castro, Joseph Stalin, Mao Zedong, Adolf Hitler and Idi Amin tried to disarm the populace before imposing governmental control. Such domination could occur in America in the not-too-distant future if we are not vigilant. We must be reasonable and willing to engage in conversation

about how to limit the availability of dangerous weapons to criminals and very violent or insane people. In light of past worldwide atrocities committed by tyrants, though, to threaten the Second Amendment rights of ordinary American citizens is itself insanity. Those wishing to ban all assault weapons fail to understand the original intent of the Second Amendment."—The Washington Times, April 23, 2014

"Our Founders did, however, recognize there was a possibility that an overbearing government drunk with power, might not submit to the will of the people and might, in fact, employ the military to suppress the will of the people. This is one of the reasons why the Second Amendment was added. It reads as follows: 'A well-regulated militia, being necessary to the security of a free State, the right of the people to keep and bear arms, shall not be infringed.' They knew that an armed populace would be a powerful deterrent to the imposition of dictatorial powers. As a testimony to their wisdom, a historical analysis informs us that many dictators, such as Hitler, Stalin, Castro, and Chairman Mao, among others confiscated firearms before their reigns of terror began."—One Vote, page 4

"Everyone in America should understand the significance of the Second Amendment to the Constitution. It gives the citizenry the right to own and bear arms. It is important for citizens to be able to aid the military in the event of a foreign invasion—however unlikely that might seem in the twenty-first century. And just as important, lawful people have the right to defend themselves against individual aggression—or their own corrupt governments. Any politician willing to ignore the Second Amendment to win votes should be regarded

with suspicion. (The same goes for any other part of the U.S. Constitution.)—One Vote, page 41

Servants Behaving as Rulers

"...the most offensive thing of all to anyone with a sense of justice is a provision [regarding Obamacare by the president] that will extend government subsidies to members of Congress and their staffs to defray their health care costs while the people they represent must suffer the slings and arrows of this outrageous program forced upon them through a host of backroom deals that would shame a mobster. Some of these representatives, unwilling to accept the deal for themselves, were actually complicit in forcing Obamacare on all Americans without even reading it. This is the height of irresponsibility, and it is hard to imagine how anyone claiming to represent the interest of their constituents could even look at themselves in the mirror if they are guilty of such actions."—The Washington Times, August 21, 2013

Taxes

"There is nothing fair about a tax code that is so complex that it is virtually impossible to comply with every aspect of the thousands of pages of rules and regulations. Because of the complexity of this code, the government can target virtually anyone and find a mistake in their tax documents, which can be used to extort money or worse. We are talking of nothing less than the precursor of a totalitarian government. Many alternative forms of taxation are used throughout the world, but the model that appeals most to me is based on biblical tithing. Under that system, everyone was required to pay one-tenth of their income to the designated authorities of the theocracy. You were not excused

if you experienced a crop failure, nor were you asked to pay triple tithes if you had a bumper crop. Under this system, the man with the bumper crop obviously would pay a lot more in tithes than the man who experienced the crop failure. If we bring this concept forward to modern times and use the 10 percent model—although it could be any percentage—a Wall Street wizard who makes $10 billion a year would have to pay $1 billion, whereas a schoolteacher who makes $50,000 a year would have to contribute $5,000. Some would say this system would not be fair because it doesn't hurt the billionaire as much as it hurts the teacher. The problem with this line of reasoning is that no one can be completely objective in determining exactly how much each person should be hurt. Proportionality eliminates this dilemma and simplifies things to the point where we don't need complex agencies such as the IRS. Instead of trying to decide how much we need to hurt the billionaire, we should be grateful that his contributions are building roads and keeping bridges in good repair proportionately as much as the contributions of hundreds of teachers. Of course, the teachers are making other important contributions to society, and we recognize this by giving everybody the same rights regardless of their financial status. The other big plus for this proportional system of taxation is that everyone is included."

"...if everyone is included in the tax base, it forces the government to be more frugal with the taxpayers' money. Officials must answer to everyone, especially when they propose tax hikes."—The Washington Times, July 17, 2013

Traditional Moral Values

"We have to be just as proactive as the secular progressives who have put us in the position we are now in."—Newsmax, June 2014

"I believe one of the reasons our nation prospered was a strong emphasis on traditional family values that included instruction on the difference between right and wrong, teaching that began in the home and continued at school. And one of the central sources for defining values was the Bible, which back then was found in all public schools. Basic religious principles were taught in public schools in such a way as to have the broadest possible application without favoring any particular denomination. Children were taught that there was a Creator to whom they were responsible and that there was a moral code given to us by the Creator to whom we would all have to answer in the afterlife. The founding fathers had much to say regarding the morality of our nation and how important it was to our future, but I think one of the best quotes that summarizes their feelings is from John Adams when he said, 'Our Constitution was made only for a moral and religious people. It is wholly inadequate to the government of any other.'"—America the Beautiful, page 105

Tea Party

"...the Tea Party was not simply an arm of the Republican Party, but rather a significant force for real change. Its constituents recognized that both the Democrats and the Republicans were responsible for excessive spending, incessant pork barrel projects to benefit special constituent groups, and intrusion into the private lives of citizens.—America the Beautiful, page 23

United States Constitution

"The Constitution was written primarily to protect the rights of the people and not the right of the government to rule the people. It restrains the natural tendencies of government to expand while disregarding the rights of its constituents. Our freedoms are safe as long as we abide by its principles."—One Nation, page 172

"I believe that the only thing that will correct our downward trajectory is the rekindling of the enthusiasm for individual freedom and the reestablishment of the U.S. Constitution as the dominant document of governance. Unless the majority of Americans awaken from their complacency and recognize the threat to their fundamental individual liberties imposed by continued expansion of the federal government, nothing will save us from the fate of all pinnacle nations that have preceded us, those that tolerated political and moral corruption while ignoring fiscal irresponsibility.—One Nation, page 176

Voter Fraud

"I have yet to find a nation that does not require some type of official voter identification card or mechanism to ensure that voters are who they say they are."—Newsmax, June 2014

"Manipulators will claim that their opponents are trying to suppress the vote by demanding identification cards in areas where they fear they won't do well electorally. I have visited many non-white countries, if you will, in the last few years, and all of them require voter identification before anyone casts a ballot. Surely these nations aren't racist?"—One Vote, page 39

"...how should we deal with voter fraud and computer hackers attempting to alter results of elections? Some claim that this does not occur in any substantial way in the United States, which is like a burglar saying that theft is rare in order to discourage the placement of security measures."— The Washington Times, July 24, 2013

War on Women

"Attempting to characterize love and compassion for human life as a 'war on women' is deceitful and pathetic. We the people must stop allowing ourselves to be manipulated by those with agendas that do not include regard for the sanctity of life. You know, there are those ... who have told women that there's a war on them because that cute little baby inside of them, they may want to get rid of it and there are people that are keeping you from doing that. There is no war on them [women]; the war is on their babies, babies that cannot defend themselves. Over the past few decades, we have destroyed 55 million of them. And we have the nerve to call other societies of the past heathen." — The Washington Times, January 22, 2014

Welfare

"A truly moral nation enacts policies that encourage personal responsibility and discourages self-destructive behavior by not subsidizing people who live irresponsibly and make poor choices. This can be done in a compassionate way by phasing out government assistance for those already receiving it and by making it clear that there will be no government assistance in the future in these situations. That is not to say that the affected individuals cannot be aided by their families, churches, and other charitable organizations and individuals. What we have just

discussed may seem a bit harsh to many bleeding heart do-gooders, but I submit that what is harsh is continuing to encourage irresponsible behavior and generating a permanent underclass."— America the Beautiful, *page 106*

"One logical and compassionate solution to the problem of growing welfare rolls is to set a date several years away for the elimination of welfare payments for able-bodied individuals who could work and support themselves."—One Nation, page 161

"There are deep and sometimes hostile divisions between those who believe in God and those who are atheists. Even deeper divisions exist between those who believe in personal responsibility and those who believe that there is no problem with government dependency."—One Nation, page 175

Chapter 10
The Speech

On February 7, 2013, Dr. Benjamin Carson, renowned pediatric neurosurgeon and a respected man of God, gave the following keynote address to the National Prayer Breakfast. President Barack Obama and First Lady, Michelle Obama were seated at the dais, as well as Vice President Joe Biden.

"Thank you so much. Mr. President, Mr. Vice President, Mrs. Obama, distinguished guests – which includes everybody. Thank you so much for this wonderful honor to be at this stage again. I was here 16 years ago, and the fact that they invited me back means that I didn't offend too many people, so that was great.

I want to start by reading four texts which will put into context what I'm going to say.

Proverbs 11:9 With his mouth the Godless destroys his neighbor, but through knowledge the righteous escapes.
Proverbs 11:12 A man who lacks judgment derides his neighbor, but a man of understanding holds his tongue.
Proverbs 11:25 A generous man will prosper. He who refreshes others will himself, be refreshed.
2nd Chronicles 7:14 If my people who are called by my name will humble themselves and pray and seek my face and turn from their wicked ways, then will I hear from heaven and will forgive their sins and heal their land.

You know, I have an opportunity to speak in a lot of venues. This is my fourth speech this week and I have an opportunity to talk to a lot of people. And I've been asking people what concerns you? What are you most concerned about in terms of the spirituality and the direction of our nation and our world? And I've talked to very prominent Democrats, very prominent Republicans. And I was surprised by the uniformity of their answers. And those have informed my comments this morning. Now, it's not my intention to offend anyone. I have discovered, however, in recent years that it's very difficult to speak to a large group of people these days and not offend someone.

And people walk away with their feelings on their shoulders waiting for you to say something, ah, did you hear that? The PC police are out in force at all times. I remember once I was talking about the difference between a human brain and a dog's brain, and a man got offended. You can't talk about dogs like that. People focus in on that, completely miss the point of what you're saying. And we've reached the point where people are afraid to actually talk about what they want to say because somebody might be offended. People are afraid to say Merry Christmas at Christmas time. Doesn't matter whether the person you're talking to is Jewish or, you know, whether they're any religion. That's a salutation, a greeting of goodwill. We've got to get over this sensitivity. You know, and it keeps people from saying what they really believe.

You know, I'm reminded of a very successful young businessman, and he loved to buy his mother these exotic gifts for mother's day. And he ran out of ideas, and then he ran across these birds. These birds were cool, you know? They cost

$5,000 apiece. They could dance, they could sing, they could talk. He was so excited, he bought two of them. Sent them to his mother, couldn't wait to call her up on mother's day, mother, mother, what'd you think of those birds? And she said, they were good. He said, no, no, no! Mother, you didn't eat those birds? Those birds cost $5,000 apiece! They could dance, they could sing, they could talk! And she said, well, they should have said something. And, you know, that's where we end up, too, if we don't speak up for what we believe. And, you know, what we need to do — what we need to do in this PC world is forget about unanimity of speech and unanimity of thought, and we need to concentrate on being respectful to those people with whom we disagree.

And that's when I believe we begin to make progress. And one last thing about political correctness, which I think is a horrible thing, by the way. I'm very, very compassionate, and I'm never out to offend anyone. But PC is dangerous. Because, you see, one of the founding principles [of this country] was freedom of thought and freedom of expression. And it muffles people. It puts a muzzle on them. And at the same time, keeps people from discussing important issues while the fabric of this society is being changed. And we cannot fall for that trick. And what we need to do is start talking about things, talking about things that are important.

Things that were important in the development of our nation. One of those things was education. I'm very passionate about education because it's made such a big difference in my life. But here we are at a time in the world, the information age, the age of technology, and yet 30% of people who enter high school in this country do not graduate. 44% of people who start a four-year college program do not finish it in four years. What is that about? Think back to a darker time in this our history. Two hundred years ago when slavery was going on it was illegal to educate a slave, particularly to teach them to read. Why do you think that was? Because when you educate a man, you liberate a man. And there I was as a youngster placing myself in the same situation that a horrible institution did because I wasn't taking advantage of the education. I was a horrible student. Most of my classmates thought I was the stupidest person in the world. They called me dummy. I was the butt of all the jokes. Now, admittedly, it was a bad environment. Single-parent home, you know, my mother and father had gotten divorced early on.

My mother got married when she was 13. She was one of 24 children. Had a horrible life. Discovered that her husband was a bigamist, had another family. And she only had a third grade education. She had to take care of us. Dire poverty. I had a horrible temper, poor self-esteem. All the things that you think would preclude success. But I had something very important, I had a mother who believed in me, and I had a mother who would never allow herself to be a victim no matter what happened. Never made excuses, and she never accepted an excuse from us. And if we ever came up with an excuse, she always said do you have a brain? And if the answer was, yes, then she said then you could have thought your way out of it. It doesn't matter what John or Susan or Mary or anybody else did or said. And it was the most important thing she did for my brother and myself. Because if you don't accept excuse, pretty soon people stop giving them, and they start looking for solutions. And that is a critical issue when it comes to success.

Well, you know, we did live in dire poverty, and one of the things that I hated was poverty. You know, some people hate spiders, some people hate snakes, I hated poverty. I couldn't stand it. But, you know, my mother couldn't stand the fact that we were doing poorly in school, and she prayed and asked God to give her wisdom, what could she do to make her sons understand the importance of wisdom? God gave her wisdom. At least in her opinion. It was to turn off the TV, let us watch only two or three programs during the week, and read two books apiece and submit to her written book reports which she couldn't read, but we didn't know that. She put check marks and highlights and stuff — But, you know, I just hated this. And my friends were out having a good time. Her friends would criticize her. They would say you can't make boys stay in the house reading books, they'll grow up and hate you. And I would overhear them and say, you know, mother, they're right, but she didn't care.

You know, after a while, I actually began to enjoy reading those books because we were very poor, but between the covers of those books I could go anywhere, I could be anybody, I could do anything. I began to read about people of great accomplishment, and as I read those stories, I began to see a connecting thread. I began to see that the person who has the most to do with you and what happens to you in life is you. You make decisions. You decide how much energy you want to put behind that decision. And I came to

*understand that I had control of my own destiny.
And at that point I didn't hate poverty anymore,
because I knew it was only temporary. I knew I
could change that. It was incredibly liberating for
me, made all the difference.*

*To continue on that theme of education, in 1831
Alexis de Tocqueville came to study America. The
Europeans were fascinated. How could a fledgling
nation, barely 50 years old already be competing
with them on virtually every level. This was
impossible. De Tocqueville was going to sort it out
and he looked at our government and he was duly
impressed by the three branches of government –
four now because now we have special interest
groups, but it was only three back in those days.
He said, WOW, this is really something, but then
he said, but let me look at their educational system
and he was blown away. See, anybody who had
finished the second grade was completely literate.
He could find a mountain man on the outskirts of
society who could read the newspaper and have a
political discussion, could tell him how the
government worked.*

*If you really want to be impressed, take a look at
the chapter on education in my latest book,
America the Beautiful, which I wrote with my wife
– it came out last year, and in that education
chapter you will see questions extracted from a
sixth grade exit exam from the 1800's – a test you
had to pass to get your sixth grade certificate. I
doubt most college graduates today could pass
that test. We have dumbed things down to that
level and the reason that is so dangerous is
because the people who founded this nation said
that our system of government was designed for a
well-informed and educated populace, and when*

they become less informed, they become vulnerable. Think about that. That is why education is so vitally important.

Now some people say, ahhh, you're over blowing it, things aren't that bad, and you're a doctor, a neurosurgeon. Why are you concerned about these things? Got news for you. FIVE doctors signed the Declaration of Independence. Doctors were involved in the framing of the Constitution, the Bill of Rights, in a whole bunch of things. It's only been since recent decades that we've extracted ourselves, which I think is a big mistake.

We need doctors, we needs scientists, engineers. We need all those people involved in government, not just lawyers... I don't have anything against lawyers, but you know, here's the thing about lawyers... I'm sorry, but I got to be truthful...– what do lawyers learn in law school? To win, by hook or by crook. You gotta win, so you got all these Democrat lawyers, and you got all these Republican lawyers and their sides want to win. We need to get rid of that. What we need to start thinking about is, how do we solve problems?

Now, before I get shot, let me finish. I don't like to bring up problems without coming up with solutions. My wife and I started the Carson Scholars Fund 16 years ago after we heard about an international survey looking at the ability of eight graders in 22 countries to solve math and science problems, and we came out No. 21 out of 22. We only barely beat out Number 22 – very concerning.

We'd go to these schools and we'd see all these trophies: State Basketball, State Wrestling, this, that and the other. The quarterback was the Big

Man on Campus. What about the intellectual Superstar? What did they get? A National Honor Society pin? A pat on the head, there, there little Nerd? Nobody cared about them. And is it any wonder that sometimes the smart kids try to hide? They don't want anybody to know they are smart? This is not helping us or our nation, so we started giving out scholarships from all backgrounds for superior academic performance and demonstration of humanitarian qualities. Unless you cared about other people, it didn't matter how smart you were. We've got plenty of people like that. We don't need smart people who don't care about other people.

We would give them money. The money would go into a Trust. They would get interest on it. When they would go to college they would get the money, but also the school gets a trophy, every bit as impressive as a sports trophy – right out there with the others. They get a medal. They get to go to a banquet. We try to put them on a pedestal as impressive as we do the all-state athletes. I have nothing against athletics or entertainment. I'm from Baltimore. The Ravens won. This is great – okay. But, but – what will maintain our position in the world? The ability to shoot a 25 foot jump shot or the ability to solve a quadratic equation? We need to put the things into proper perspective.

Many teachers have told us that when we put a Carson Scholar in their classroom, the GPA of the whole classroom goes up over the next year. It's been very gratifying. We started 16 years ago with 25 scholarships in Maryland, now we've given out more than 5,000 and we are in all 50 states, but we've also put in Reading Rooms. These are fascinating places that no little kid could possibly pass up. And, they get points for the amount of time they spend reading, and the number of books they read. They can trade the points for prizes. In the beginning they do it for the prizes, but it doesn't take long before their academic performance begins to improve.

And we particularly target Title One schools where the kids come from homes with no books and they go to schools with no libraries. Those are the ones who drop out. We need to truncate that process early on because we can't afford to waste any of those young people. You know, for every one of those people we keep from going down that path – that path of self-destruction and mediocrity, that's one less person you have to protect yourself and your family from. One less person you have to pay for in the penal or welfare system. One more taxpaying productive member of society who may invent a new energy source or come up with a cure for cancer. They are all important to us and we need every single one of them it makes a difference. And when you go home tonight read about it, Carson Scholars, carsonscholars.org.

Why is it so important that we educate our people? Because we don't want to go down the pathway as so many pinnacle nations that have preceded us. I think particularly about ancient Rome. Very powerful. Nobody could even challenge them militarily, but what happened to them? They destroyed themselves from within. Moral decay, fiscal irresponsibility. They destroyed themselves. If you don't think that can happen to America, you get out your books and you start reading, but you know, we can fix it.

Why can we fix it because we're smart. We have some of the most intellectually gifted people leading our nation. All we need to do is remember what our real responsibilities are so that we can solve the problems. I think about these problems all the time, and my role, you know, model was Jesus. He used parables to help people understand things. And one of our big problems right now, and like I said, I'm not politically correct, so I'm sorry, but you know – our deficit is a big problem. Think about it. And our National Debt – 16.5 trillion dollars – you think that's not a lot of money? I'll tell you what! Count one number per second, which you can't even do because once you get to a thousand it will take you longer than a second, but...one number per second. You know how long it would take you to count to 16 Trillion? 507,000 years – more than a half a million years to get there. We have to deal with this.

Here's a parable: A family falls on hard times. Dad loses his job or is demoted to part time work. He has 5 children. He comes to the 5 children, he says we're going to have to reduce your allowance. Well, they're not happy about it but – he says, except for John and Susan.   They're, they're special. They get to keep their allowance. In fact, we'll give them more. How do you think that's going to go down? Not too well. Same thing happens. Enough said.

What about our taxation system?   So complex there is no one who can possibly comply with every jot and tittle of our tax system. If I wanted to get you, I could get you on a tax issue. That doesn't make any sense. What we need to do is come up with something that is simple.

When I pick up my Bible, you know what I see? I see the fairest individual in the Universe, God, and he's given us a system. It's called tithe. Now we *don't necessarily have to do it 10% but it's principle. He didn't say, if your crops fail, don't give me any tithes. He didn't say, if you have a bumper crop, give me triple tithes. So there must be something inherently fair about proportionality. You make 10 billion dollars you put in a Billion. You make $10 you put in $1 – of course, you gotta get rid of the loopholes, but now some people say, that's not fair because it doesn't hurt the guy who made 10 billion dollars as much as the guy who made $10. Where does it say you have to hurt the guy? He's just put in a billion in the pot. We don't need to hurt him.*

It's that kind of thinking – it's that kind of thinking that has resulted in 602 banks in the Cayman Islands. That money needs to be back here, building our infrastructure and creating jobs – and we're smart enough – we're smart enough to figure out how to do that.

We've already started down the path to solving one of the other big problems, health care. We need to have good health care for everybody. It's the most important thing that a person can have. Money means nothing, titles mean nothing when you don't have your health, but we've got to figure out efficient ways to do it. We spend a lot of money on health care, twice as much per capita as anybody in else in the world, and yet not very efficient. What can we do?

Here's my solution. When a person is born, give him a birth certificate, an electronic medical record and a health savings account [HSA], to which money can be contributed, pre-tax from the time you are born, to the time you die. When you die, you can pass it on to your family members so that when you're 85 years old and you've got 6 diseases, you're not trying to spend up everything. You're happy to pass it on and nobody is talking about death panels. That's number one.

Also –

For the people who are indigent, who don't have any money, we can make contributions to their HSA each month because we already have this huge pot of money instead of sending it to bureaucracy – let's put it into HSAs. Now they have some control over their own health care and what do you think they're going to do? They're going to learn very quickly how to be responsible. When Mr. Jones gets that diabetic foot ulcer, he's not going to the Emergency Room and blowing a big chunk of it. He's going to go to the Clinic. He learns that very quickly – gets the same treatment. In the Emergency Room they send him out. In the Clinic they say, now let's get your diabetes under control so that you're not back here in three weeks with another problem. That's how we begin to solve these kinds of problems. It's much more complex than that, and I don't have time to go into it all, but we can do all these things because we are smart people.

And let me begin to close here – another parable: Sea Captain, and he's out on the sea near the area where the Titanic went down. And they look ahead and there's a bright light right there – another ship he figures. He tells his signaler to signal that ship: deviate 10 degrees to the South. Back comes the message, no you deviate 10 degrees to the North. Well, he's a little bit incensed, you know. He says, send a message, this is Captain Johnson, deviate 10 degrees to the South. Back comes the message, this is Ensign 4th Class Reilly. Deviate 10 degrees to the North.

Now Captain Johnson is really upset. He says send him a message, this is a Naval Destroyer. Back comes the message, this is a Lighthouse. Enough said.

Now, what about the symbol of our Nation? The eagle, the bald eagle. It's an interesting story how we chose that but a lot of people think we call it the bald eagle because it looks like it has a bald head. That's not the reason. It comes from the Old English word Piebald, which means crowned with white. And we just shortened it to bald. Now, use that the next time you see somebody who thinks they know everything. You'll get 'em on that one.

But, why is that eagle able to fly, high, forward? Because it has two wings: a left wing and a right wing. Enough said.

And I want to close with this story: two hundred years ago this Nation was involved in a war, the War of 1812. The British, who are now our good friends thought that we were young whippersnappers. It was time for us to become a colony again. They were winning that war and marching up the Eastern Seaboard, destroying city after city, destroying Washington, D.C., burned down the White House. Next stop Baltimore. As they came into the Chesapeake Bay, there were armadas of war ships as far as the eye could see. It was looking grim. Fort McHenry standing right there. General Armisted, who was in charge of Fort McHenry, had a large American flag commissioned to fly in front of the Fort. The Admiral in charge of the British Fleet was offended, said take that flag down. You have until dusk to take that Flag down. If you don't take it down, we will reduce you to ashes.

There was a young amateur poet on board by the name of Francis Scott Key, sent by President Madison to try to obtain the release of an American physician who was being held captive. He overheard the British plans. They were not going to let him off the ship. He mourned. As dusk approached he mourned for his fledgling young nation, and as the sun fell, the bombardment started. Bombs bursting in air. Missiles, so much debris. He strained, trying to see, was the flag still there? Couldn't see a thing. All night long it continued. At the crack of dawn he ran out to the bannister. He looked straining his eyes all he could only see dust and debris.

Then there was a clearing and he beheld the most beautiful sight he had ever seen – the torn and tattered Stars and Stripes still waving. And many historians say that was the turning point in the War of 1812. We went on to win that war and to retain our freedom and if you had gone onto the grounds of Fort McHenry that day, you would have seen at the base of that flag, the bodies of soldiers who took turns. Propping up that flag, they would not let that flag go down because they believed in what that flag symbolized. And what did it symbolize? One nation, under God, indivisible, with liberty and justice for all. Thank you. God Bless."

Chapter 11
What You Can Do!

I hope that by now you are as enthusiastic about the candidacy of Ben Carson as I am. Few times in history do American voters have an opportunity to elect a truly great president. And, considering the dire circumstances our nation is now in, that is exactly what we need, a man who will be a truly great president. The mess that the current administration has created and the direction they have taken calls for a president with great fortitude, strong principles, and a man humble enough to rely on God to lead him in the right direction.

If you want to elect Ben Carson President in 2016, here are ten things you can do right now to help make that happen...

1. **Pray.** I believe there is nothing as powerful as prayer. The Bible tells us that... *"Prayers offered by those who have God's approval are effective."* (James 5:16 GWN). Make no mistake about it, the candidacy of Ben Carson is a long shot, but *"If God is for us, who can be against us?"* (Romans 8:32 GWN). And, if you want to smile when you are praying, just remember that there is a reason that Ben Carson's colleagues called him *"Longshot."* [147]

2. **Tell.** Tell your friends, relatives, acquaintances, and neighbors (FRANs) about Ben Carson. You have in your hands the ammunition you need to make the case for Ben Carson. Tell them about his courage in speaking at the National Prayer Breakfast, his faith, his dedication to our Constitution, his

trustworthiness, his incredible life story, why he can win, and why he will make a great president.

3. **Donate.** Go to www.2016Committee.org and donate to help nominate and elect Ben Carson as the next President of the United States. Your dollars are critical to nominating and electing Ben Carson as our next president. Just as Barack Obama started years before the 2008 election, we must work hard now to put Ben Carson in the White House. If you don't want to donate online, make your check payable to: The 2016 Committee, and mail to Post Office Box 1351, Merrifield, VA 22116-1351.

4. **Volunteer.** Go to www.2016Committee.org and sign on as a volunteer. You'll learn about what you can do in your own community to get the band wagon rolling for Ben Carson. The 2016 Committee has volunteer organizations in each one of the fifty states. We have regional coordinators and state chairmen in almost every state. In fact, in the early delegate selection states we have a county chairman in virtually every county. Let them know you are willing to volunteer. They will welcome you with open arms.

5. **Write.** Send an e-mail or letter to your local newspaper and tell them why Ben Carson is the best choice for the GOP in 2016. Remind them that Ben Carson is sure to win, will heal our nation, and is a trustworthy conservative. Include a quote from Ben Carson on a hot topic. You can use one of the quotes enclosed.

6. **Call.** Call in to your local talk radio show and speak up for Ben Carson. You can do this. Tell them the Ben Carson story. Explain why he is the right candidate for the GOP in 2016. Tell them that

the polls have him in first or second place and that support for Ben Carson is growing.

7. **Read.** Buy a copy of one of Ben Carson's best-selling books, *America the Beautiful*, or *One Nation*. Both of these books are written by Ben Carson (along with his wife Candy). Each of these books tells of Ben Carson's passion for America and what he wants to do to return our nation to greatness. And, if you want to know more about his incredible life, read *Gifted Hands*, the story of his rise from poverty to become a world renowned pediatric neurosurgeon. Giving a FRAN one of these books is a great way to introduce them to Ben Carson. You can purchase a copy of these books at www.amazon.com.

8. **Visit.** Visit GOP and activist group meetings in your area. Go to the lunch clubs, GOP women's clubs, tea party groups, and GOP men's clubs. Introduce yourself and make the three main points, Ben Carson will win, Ben Carson will heal, and Ben Carson is a trustworthy conservative. If you have never before been active in the Republican Party, now is the time to do so. It's the only game in town for conservatives and they will welcome you with open arms.

9. **Advertise.** Advertise and promote the candidacy of Ben Carson by putting a bumper strip or magnet sign on your car and a yard sign in your yard. You can find all of these at www.2016Committee.org. Encourage other Ben Carson supporters to put a sign on their car and even a sign up in their yard. You can help get the word out!

10. **Show Up.** The world is run by those who show up! The first state to select delegates to the national

Republican presidential nominating convention is Iowa, but your state convention, caucus or primary won't be far behind. In many states, you cannot vote in the GOP primary without changing your party registration to Republican. In no state can you run for a county, district, state or national GOP delegate position without being affiliated with the Republican Party. Check your state laws. Our goal is to get a majority of delegate votes at the Republican National Convention in 2016 to nominate Dr. Ben Carson and then support him through the fall general election to victory. Get ready for the nominating process now by changing your party affiliation (if necessary) and/or making yourself indispensable to your local GOP. Look into becoming a delegate to your 2015 county, district, and state convention. This is not as hard as you may think. Remember, the GOP folks will welcome you with open arms. Once you attend a local convention or caucus, you will know the ropes and may be able to help someone go to the national convention in 2016 as a Carson delegate...or even go yourself!

Ronald Reagan defeated an incumbent Democrat president, Jimmy Carter, and his coattails brought about Republican control of the United States Senate in 1980. It didn't happen by accident. Americans from all across the nation donated to his campaign, and tens of thousands of volunteers made telephone calls and walked door-to-door in their neighborhoods in support of his candidacy. You and I are members of the army behind Ben Carson. We love our nation. We revere our Founders. We believe in the United States Constitution. We trust in God. And, we believe in maximum individual freedom.

Just as our forefathers were called upon to act in order to save our nation from the tyranny of King George III, and generations following them fought to preserve the United States of America, this is our time to act. With courage, boldness, and humbleness, we must fight for freedom for ourselves, our children, and our children's children. May God grant us the victory!

Acknowledgments

Clearly my greatest debt in writing this book is to Dr. Benjamin Solomon Carson about whom and from whom I have learned so much. Through his writings, his speeches, and most important of all, the way he has lived his life, I have learned what it means to be a man of character in the 21st century. Dr. Carson has not only awakened millions of Americans to the dire threats facing our nation, but also to the opportunities of citizens to exercise their power in the political process. He has introduced ideas and set forth policies that can return America to greatness, and in doing so he has ignited a nationwide movement to elect him as the next president of the United States. This book would have neither been possible, nor necessary had it not been for the willingness of Ben Carson to make the sacrifice of offering himself as a candidate for President of the United States.

This is the third book that I have written, the first two being books about my great grandfather, John Philip Sousa, the world renowned *March King*. Although I never met him, he has served as an inspiration to me throughout my life to not only give my best, but also to cherish the United States of America as the greatest and most generous nation in the world. I believe that were he alive today he would be leading marches and parades on behalf of Ben Carson. He was a man who felt privileged to be an American, and he never took that blessing for granted. His love for America has been passed from generation to generation and it stirs me yet today.

Many individuals helped to make this book possible, including Bruce Eberle, who not only donated the services of Kaleidoscope Publishing, Ltd., but also provided ideas, insight, and other significant contributions that made the writing and publication of this book possible. I would also be remiss if I did not specifically thank Kristine Herrick at Kaleidoscope for her tireless efforts working with printers and others to make publication of this book timely and inexpensive enough to give it wide circulation. Also, at Kaleidoscope, I would like to thank Karen London, Bill Griffiths and Brian Anderson, who assisted this project over many hurdles. I would also like to thank Andy Hall, who designed the cover of this book. Andy, you did a spectacular job.

Many individuals spent hours reading the manuscript of this book and made corrections. I am indebted to them for their painstaking proofreading efforts. These individuals include Mari Pierce, Sherry Dopp, Kathi Eberle, Pam Thomas, John Livingstone, and my good friend, Allen Brandstater, who made many sound and wise suggestions for the improvement of this book which I had the good sense to incorporate. I am also indebted to Declan Bransfield and Vernon Robinson for research assistance and support.

Another person indispensable to the publication of this book is Tammy Cali, President of the Eberle Communications Group, Inc. Tammy cleared away roadblocks, provided wise counsel, and pushed this project forward to publication. Thank you, Tammy.

I, of course, want to thank my dear wife, Catherine, for her support of my role as the National Chairman of the National Draft Ben Carson for President Committee (now The 2016 Committee) and my always forgiving and understanding pal, Romeo, head of canines for Carson.

On a personal note, let me say that writing a book is, for me at least, a daunting challenge. The story and the message come easily, but organizing it into some sort of understandable order, and making sure the documentation is properly credited and the index is extensive enough to be worthwhile to the reader take patience and perseverance. For that patience and perseverance I thank the United States Air Force in which I had the honor of serving for a number of years. Without the discipline that I acquired from my time in the USAF, I do not believe I would have ever undertaken writing this book. It is my hope that you have found it to be valuable and worth the time you took to read it.

Pro Gloria Dei!

Recommended Reading

To know more about Dr. Benjamin Carson and where he stands on the important issues of the day, read his books…

America the Beautiful
Zondervan, © 2012 Benjamin
Carson and Candy Carson

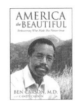

Gifted Hands
The Ben Carson Story
Zondervan, © 1990 Review &
Herald Publishing Association

One Nation
Sentinel, © 2014 American
Business Collaborative, LLC

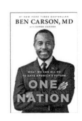

One Vote
Tyndale House Publishers, Inc., ©
2014 Benjamin S. Carson, Sr., MD

Endnotes

Chapter 1: Ben Carson the Man

[1] Benjamin Carson, *Take the Risk, Learning to Identify, Choose, and Live with Acceptable Risk* (Grand Rapids: Zondervan 2008) p. 85
[2] Ibid, p. 86
[3] Ibid, p. 149
[4] This is an estimate based on the following information. As defined by the American Academy of Pediatrics, pediatric care begins with pre-natal and continues through the age of 21. According to the U.S. Centers for Disease Control and Prevention approximately 1.1 million Americans are treated for Traumatic Brain Injury (TBI) each year. CDC notes that 475,000 children, ages 9 to 14, suffer from TBI each year (note that this statistic does not cover pediatric care between the ages of 15 and 21). According to that statistic it is reasonable to conclude that approximately 50% of all TBI occurs in children between the ages of 9 to 21. Johns Hopkins Children's Center consistently ranks among the top three hospitals in neurology and neurosurgery. According to information provided by Johns Hopkins department of Neurology and Neurosurgery they *"provide over 30,000 outpatient consultations and perform more than 4,000 brain, tumor, vascular, and peripheral nerve operations"* each year. The typical cost of brain surgery in the United States costs between $50,000 and $150,000 depending on the hospital, and the type of surgery. It is reasonable to assume that considering its high ranking, Johns Hopkins University Hospital would be among the more expensive places to have brain surgery. Nevertheless, if you assume a median brain surgery cost of $100,000, ignore the revenue from outpatient consultations and assume half of the 4,000 brain surgeries performed at Johns Hopkins were performed in the pediatric division headed by Dr. Carson, the total annual amount of billings for brain surgery would be $200 million per year.
[5] Carson Scholars Fund, Inc. (http://carsonscholars.org) 305 W. Chesapeake Avenue, Suite 310, Towson, MD 21204

6 Daniel Foster, "Five Things You Didn't Know About Dr. Carson," *National Review Online*, February 13, 2013, www.nationalreview.com/articles/340618/five-things-you-didn-t-know-about-dr-carson-daniel-foster/page/0/1?splash=

7 Ben Carson. (2014). The Biography.com website. Retrieved 02:26, Nov 10, 2014, from http://www.biography.com/people/ben-carson-475422

8 http://en.wikipedia.org/wiki/Ben_Carson

9 Frank Rich, "Sixth Most Admired Man in America," *New York Times Magazine*, February 24, 2015

10 Andrew Prokop, "Poll: The Only Presidential Contender More Popular than Hillary Clinton is Ben Carson," *Vox*, www.vox.com/2015/3/13/8207935/hillary-clinton-favorability March 13, 2015

11 *Gifted Hands* movie, Sony Pictures Television, Inc., 2009

12 Benjamin Carson, *Gifted Hands* (Grand Rapids: Zondervan 1990), back cover

13 Ben Carson's 2013 National Prayer Breakfast speech, Reprinted in its entirety in chapter 10 of this book

14 Ben Carson, "Political Correctness and the Slavery of Obamacare,"*The Washington Times*, March 18, 2014

15 *A Time for Choosing,* Ronald Reagan's speech on behalf of the presidential candidacy of Barry Goldwater, Los Angeles, California, October 27, 1964

Chapter 2: Why Ben Carson Will Win

16 David Robertson, *Sly and Able, A Political Biography of James F. Byrnes*, (New York, W.W. Norton & Company, Inc., 1994), p. 92

17 Barry Goldwater desegregated the Goldwater stores before most other stores in Phoenix, he made contributions to the NAACP and the Urban League, and as a member of the Phoenix city council, was instrumental in desegregating Phoenix public schools, and, as a Reserve Major General in the Arizona Air National Guard, desegregated that organization more than a year before president Harry Truman gave the order to desegregate the military.

[18] Siobhan Hughes, "Wall Street Journal, GOP Bid for Black Vote Faces Hurdles," *Wall Street Journal,* October 24, 2014
[19] See endnote 9
[20] Related to author by Bruce Eberle, whose company, Campaign Funding Direct provided direct mail fund raising services to the Herman Cain presidential campaign. In a November 2011 telephone conversation Eberle asked Cain Campaign Chairman Mark Block what the campaign's internal polls revealed in regard to support from African American. Block replied that they showed above 40% support from black Americans and more than 60% support from Hispanic Americans.
[21] www.AngiesList.com, Angie's List, 1030 E. Washington St., Indianapolis, IN 46202
[22] Ben Terris, "He's already a famous surgeon and author, so why is Ben Carson toying with a longshot presidential bid?" *The Washington Post*, Style Section, August 28, 2014
[23] Greg Richter, "Liberal SPLC Removes Ben Carson from 'Extremist Files,'" *Newsmax*, February 11, 2015
[24] Survey conducted by The Polling Company, founder and chairman, Kellyanne Conway on behalf of The 2016 Committee completed on March 20, 2015
[25] Blood in the soil. A reference to the blood of African Americans being spilt as they toiled as slaves; an identity within the African American community as someone who is a descendent of slaves.
[26] See endnote 12, Jesse Jackson back cover testimonial.
[27] Gallup, 2014 Ethics, Honesty/Ethics in Professions survey. The survey question: "Please tell me how you would rate the honesty and ethical standards of people in these different fields— very high, high, average, low or very low?" Nurses received an 80% vote of confidence, followed by medical doctors who received a 65% high or very high rating.
[28] Benjamin Carson and Candy Carson, *America the Beautiful*, (Grand Rapids: Zondervan 2012), p. 158
[29] Ibid, p. 156
[30] Ibid, p. 156
[31] See endnote 23
[32] See endnote 23
[33] See endnote 19

34 National Draft Ben Carson for President Campaign Director Vernon Robinson made this purchase on behalf of the super PAC. The ads targeting black voters ran for one month on the *Tom Joyner Show* which is aired on urban contemporary radio stations across the nation.

35 America's Majority Foundation exit poll of 1,600 African American voters in North Carolina, November 5-9, 2014

36 Bob Beckel, *Fox News Channel,* November 4, 2014

37 Daniel Strauss, *Talking Points Memo Online*, October 21, 2014, 4:39 PM. "On one page of the flyer, reported by the *Atlanta Journal-Constitution*, the words 'if you want to prevent another Ferguson in their future...' over a picture of two young African American children with signs that read 'don't shoot.'"

38 Phillip Cowan, "The MSM Ignores 'Run Ben Run,'" *American Thinker*, October 11, 2014

39 Uncle Tom. A derogatory term referring to a black man who acts subservient to or tries to curries favor with whites. Derived from Harriet Beecher Stowe's book, *Uncle Tom's Cabin*, published in 1852.

40 Oreo. A derogatory term whose first use is attributed to author Ralph Ellison. It refers to black person who acts like a white person, i.e. black on the outside and white on the inside like an Oreo Cookie.

41 See endnote 19

42 William Shakespeare, Merchant of Venice, Act 2, Scene 2, 1596

43 Julianne Malveaux, "I hope his wife feeds him [Clarence Thomas, Justice, U.S. Supreme Court] lots of eggs and butter and he dies early like many black men do, of heart disease. He is an absolutely reprehensible person." *USA Today*, November 4, 1994

44 Juan Williams, *The O'Reilly Factor*, Fox News Channel, October 18, 2010. Response by Williams to to a question posed by Bill O'Reilly "...when I get on the plane, I got to tell you, if I see people who are in Muslim garb and I think, you know, they are identifying themselves first and foremost as Muslims, I get worried. I get nervous."

45 Juan Williams, *Enough*, (New York: Crown Publishing Group, a division of Random House, Inc. 2006)

46 Touré Neblett, *MSNBC*, Co-host *The Cycle*, March 21, 2013

47 Leo Terrell, Civil Rights Attorney and Community Activist *Sean Hannity Show*, Fox News Channel, April 1, 2013

48 Earl Ofari Hutchinson *Huffington Post*, October 21, 2013

49 Ibid

50 Chelsi Henry, "Republicans are Winning the Support of Black Americans, This Election Was a Turning Point," *The Washington Post*, November 7, 2014

51 Remarks by nominee for Associate Justice of the United States Supreme Court, Clarence Thomas before U.S. Senate Judiciary Committee, October 1991. His complete sentence was, "This is not an opportunity to talk about difficult matters privately or in a closed environment. This is a circus. It's a national disgrace. And from my standpoint, as a black American, it is a high-tech lynching for uppity blacks who in any way deign to think for themselves, to do for themselves, to have different ideas, and it is a message that unless you kowtow to an old order, this is what will happen to you. You will be lynched, destroyed, caricatured by a committee of the U.S. Senate rather than hung from a tree.

52 Jane Mansbridge and Katherine Tate, *The Thomas Nomination in the Black Community: Race Trumps Gender*, *Political Science & Politics*, Vol. 25, No. 3, September 1992, p. 488-492. The conclusion of this report was summed up as follows, "Some who watched the hearings on the television therefore must have seen the procedure as attacking the character of a Black man who had been nominated for a great honor."

53 Ibid

54 See endnote 18

55 Voting and Registration in the Election of November 2012 – Detailed Tables, United States Census Bureau, Table 4.b. "Reported Voting and Registration, by Sex, Race, and Hispanic Origin, for States: November 2012"

56 Randall Monger and James Yankay, "U.S. Lawful Permanent Residents: 2013," Annual Flow Report, U.S. Department of Homeland Security, Office of Immigration Statistics, May 2014

57 Seth McLaughlin, "GOP Makes Inroad with Asian Voters in Midterms, " *Washington Times*, November 10, 2014

58 *How Groups Voted in 2012,* Roper Center, University of Connecticut

59 Paul Kengor, "Romney Beats McCain!," *American Spectator*, December 3, 2012

60 Seen endnote 54

61 See endnote 18

62 Ian Tuttle, "Soros-backed Super PAC Targets Allen West," *National Review Online* The Corner, July 13, 2012

63 Elisabeth Meinecke, "West Statements Make Him 'Top Democratic Target'," *Townhall.com*, April 29, 2012

64 2009 BlackDemographics.com defines middle class households as having an income of $35,000 to $100,000 per year

65 Ibid

66 See endnote 15

67 Ibid

68 Ibid

69 Former British Prime Minister Margaret Thatcher eulogy for Ronald Reagan, June 11, 2004

70 Ben Carson speech at the National Prayer Breakfast, February 13, 2013

71 "Ben Carson for President," Review & Outlook, Wall Street Journal, February 8, 2013

72 "Ben Carson Wades into Hostile Territory at Al Sharpton Event," *NewsMax*, April 8, 2015

73 Ibid

Chapter 3: How Ben Carson Will Win

74 Daniel Webster, *Discourse in Commemoration of Adams and Jefferson*, 1826

75 Matthew chapter 10, verse 16, *God's Word* translation

76 Patrick Henry, speech on the Federal Constitution, Virginia Ratifying Convention June 5, 1788

77 John Adams, notes for an oration at Braintree, Spring 1772

78 Thomas W. Jacobson, *Wisdom for Nations: Character, Virtue, Integrity, Courage*, George Washington, letter to Major-General Robert Howe August 17, 1779, International Diplomacy & Public Policy Center, September 2012

79 See endnote 18

[80] *How Groups Voted in 1980,* Roper Center, University of Connecticut

[81] *How Americans Voted in 2004,* Roper Center, University of Connecticut

[82] See endnote 54

[83] W.T. Garrett, "More than Half of Hispanics Identify as Conservative," *Dallas Morning News,* February 24, 2010

[84] Tony Lee, "Studies Show GOP Can Win Elections Opposing Amnesty in 20-14: Impact of Latino Vote Overrated," *Breitbart.com,* October 21, 2014

[85] Billy Hallowell, "Is Rejecting a Path to Citizenship for Illegal Immigrants Un-Christian," *The Blaze,* April 18, 2013

[86] Paul Taylor, Director, "Latino Voters in the 2012 Election," Pew Research Center, Pew Hispanic Center

[87] Barack Obama, Univision interview, October 25, 2010

[88] Richard Nadler, *Republican Issue Advertising in Black & Hispanic Population Areas: A Meta-Study of the 2002 Mid-Term Elections,* (Kansas City: Access Communications Group), 2003

Chapter 4: Ben Carson Will Heal Our Broken Land

[89] Abraham Lincoln, Second Inaugural Address, March 4, 1865

[90] Abraham Lincoln, last public speech, Washington, D.C., April 11, 1865

[91] Louis P. Masur, *The Civil War, A Concise History,* (New York: Oxford University Press, Inc.), 2011, p. 79

[92] Gallup poll based on telephone interviews conducted Dec. 8-11, 2014 of a random sample of 805 adults, aged 18 and older, living in all 50 U.S. states and the District of Columbia.

[93] On June 16, 1858 Abraham Lincoln was selected by the delegates to the Illinois Republican State Convention to be their candidate for the United States Senate to oppose Democrat Stephen Douglas. Upon receiving the Republican nomination, Lincoln gave his *House Divided* speech to the delegates. The idea of a divided house being unable to stand came from the gospels of Matthew, Mark, and Luke where it is recorded that Jesus said *"a kingdom divided against itself cannot stand."*

[94] Ben Carson, *All In with Chris Hayes,* MSNBC, May 24, 2014

95 Dinesh D'Souza, *America, Imagine a World Without Her* (Washington: Regnery Publishing, 2014) pp. 40-41
96 Barack Obama, Keynote address, Democrat National Convention, Boston, Massachusetts, July 27, 2004
97 Ibid
98 Ibid
99 Barack Obama, victory speech, Grant Park, Chicago, November 4, 2008
100 Rev. Martin Luther King, Jr., *I Have a Dream* speech, Lincoln Memorial, Washington, D.C., August 28, 1963
101 Barack Obama, victory speech, Grant Park, Chicago, November 4, 2008
102 Genesis 5.b., God's Word translation, 1995 God's Word translation

Chapter 5: Ben Carson: Trustworthy Conservative

103 Matthew 11:17, God's Word translation, 1995 God's Word translation
104 Ibid
105 See endnote 65
106 Ben Terris, "Ben Carson's Bully Pulpit," *The Washington Post*, August 29, 2014
107 Ben Carson, *Take the Risk* (Grand Rapids: Zondervan, 2008)
108 Ibid. p.21
109 Ibid p. 64
110 Ben Carson, *One Nation*, (New York: Sentinel, 2014) p. 139
111 Paul Kengor, *11 Principles of a Reagan Conservative*, (New York, Beaufort Books, 2014), p. 9
112 Ronald Reagan, remarks at *Georgetown University's Bicentennial Convocation*, October 1, 1988

Chapter 6: Ben Carson: Prepared to Serve

113 Related to author by Bruce Eberle who asked former United States Attorney General Edwin Meese this question on September 10, 2014
114 See endnote 100, p. 16

[115] 1 Kings, 3:5–14, God's Word translation, © 1995 God's Word translation

[116] Thomas Jones Barker painting, *The Secret of England's Greatness*, 1864

[117] See endnote 100, p. 140

[118] Reid J. Epstein, "Outsider Ben Carson Rises in 2016 GOP Field," *Wall Street Journal*, January 26, 2016

[119] Michael P. Johnson, *Reading the American Past: Volume I: To 1877: Selected Historical Documents* (Boston: Bedford/St. Martin's, 2012) p. 152

[120] Merle Sinclair, *They Signed for Us* (New York: Hawthorn Books, Inc., 1957)

[121] The phrase comes from John Winthrop's 1630 sermon *"A Model of Christian Charity"*. Winthrop admonished the future Massachusetts Bay colonists that their new community would be *"as a city upon a hill"*, watched by the world. The idea comes from Matthew 5:14, Jesus says, *"You are light for the world. A city cannot be hidden when it is located on a hill."—God's Word* translation. It was popularized by Ronald Reagan who used it numerous times, most notably in his farewell speech to the nation on January 11, 1989.

Chapter 7: A Ben Carson Presidency

[122] See endnote 13

[123] See endnote 13

[124] See endnote 100, p. 149

[125] Ben Carson, "How to Keep Ebola Out of America," *The Washington Times*, October 9, 2014

[126] Ben S. Carson, "The Face of Evil," *The Washington Times*, February 18, 2015

[127] Ben Carson, America's News Room hosted by Bill Hemmer, February 16, 2015

[128] See endnote 100, pp. 143-144

[129] See endnote 13

[130] See endnote 100, p. 70

Chapter 8: Ben Carson vs. Clinton

131 Dinesh D'Souza, *America, Imagine a World Without Her* (Washington: Regnery Publishing, 2014), p. 87
132 John Fund, *Stealing Elections* (New York: Encounter Books, 2004, 2008) p. 58
133 Saul D. Alinsky, *Rules for Radicals*, (New York: Random House, 1971), dedication page
134 See endnote 119
135 Paul Kengor, *The Communist*, (New York: Threshold Editions/Mercury Ink, 2012, p. 4 and p. 11
136 See endnote 100, p. 41
137 Ibid
138 See endnote 101, pp. 15, 16
139 Benjamin Franklin, *The Writings of Ben Franklin,* letter to the Abbés Chalut and Arnaud, April 17, 1787, Volume 9, p. 569
140 Thomas W. Jacobson, *Wisdom for Nations: Character, Virtue, Integrity, Courage*, John Adams, letter to Zabdiel Adams, June 21, 1776, International Diplomacy and Public Policy Center, Philadelphia, compiled September 2012
141 Charles Colson, *How Now Shall We Live?* (Wheaton, Tyndale House Publishers, Inc., 1999) p. 149
142 Barack Obama, 2001 interview with WBEZ, a Chicago public radio station
143 John Adams Letter to Abigail Adams 17 July 17, 1775
144 Balkanization, or Balkanisation, is a geopolitical term, originally used to describe the process of fragmentation or division of a region or state into smaller regions or states that are often hostile or non-cooperative with one another, *Wikipedia*, en.wikipedia.org/wiki/Balkanization
145 See endnote 110
146 Ben S. Carson, "The Wisdom of Peace Through Strength," *The Washington Times*, December 31, 2014

Chapter 11: What You Can Do

147 See endnote 22

Index

Index